THE BLACK CLOTH

THE BLACK CLOTH

A Collection of African Folktales

Bernard Binlin Dadié

Foreword by Es'kia Mphahlele

Translated by Karen C. Hatch

The University of Massachusetts Press

Amherst, 1987

First published in France as *Le Pagne Noir: Contes Africains*
© 1955 by Présence Africaine
Foreword, preface, and translation © 1987 by The University of Massachusetts Press
All rights reserved
Printed in the United States of America
Set in Linoterm Sabon
Printed by Cushing-Malloy and bound by John Dekker & Sons

Library of Congress Cataloging-in-Publication Data

Dadié, Bernard Binlin, 1916–
The black cloth.

Translation of: Le pagne noir.
Bibliography: p.
1. Folklore—Africa—Fiction. 2. Tales—Africa.
I. Title.
PQ3989.D28P313   1987   843   86-25043
ISBN 0-87023-556-7 (alk. paper)
ISBN 0-87023-557-5 (pbk. alk. paper)

CONTENTS

Foreword by Es'kia Mphahlele   ix

Translator's Preface   xiii

The Mirror of Dearth   3

The Black Cloth   12

The Pitcher   17

Spider's Hump   28

L'Enfant Terrible   36

Spider's Ox   43

Spider and the Tortoise   52

Mother Iguana's Funeral   62

The Pig's Snout   71

The Hunter and the Boa   82

The Sacred Cow   91

The Bat's Relations   99

The Yam Field   104

The Dowry   115

Spider and His Son   124

The Man Who Wanted to Be King   132

Other Works by Dadié   139

TRANSLATOR'S
ACKNOWLEDGMENTS

For their patience, encouragement, and help, I would like to express my sincere gratitude to Mr. Es'kia Mphahlele and Mr. Bernard Dadié. Special thanks must also go to Palmer and John.

FOREWORD

It was the decade of the fifties. A literary renaissance was on in West and South Africa. There was an awakening, and the African had found his voice.

Of course, during the thirties, the poets of negritude like Léopold Senghor and Birago and David Diop (among the Paris-based blacks from French colonies) had already begun to hammer out African imagery and symbolism in an effort to free themselves from the shackles of assimilation. But the literary upsurge of the fifties contributed even more of the African essence to the French and English languages; this was because its base was the African landscape itself.

The literary movement coincided with the realization of nationalism whose spirit had taken root in the previous decade. Already the gray dawn of independence was taking on the lurid tint of the rising sun; the bright new day would soon be upon us—*kwacha,* as the Zambians would call it, to sum up all the expectations and ecstasy of self-determination.

Bernard Dadié's was to be one of the voices that began to fill the air and express the spirit of the times. His *Climbié,* an account of African childhood, like Cheikh Hamidou Kane's *L'Aventure ambigüe* and

Camara Laye's *L'Enfant noir,* represents a genre that came to establish itself as a viable tradition on African soil. *Climbié* was later to be translated into English by Karen Chapman (now Hatch), thus making it accessible to a large segment of the continent's readership.

The writing of such chronicles of an African childhood was the authors' way of coming to terms with the questions every sensitive colonized person educated in the Western tradition would sooner or later have to ask: Who am I? Where do I come from? Where am I going? While giving poetic and fictional expression to the tensions of independence and the events that led to it, the writer realized that he would at the same time have to rediscover his oral tradition. It was a natural development of what the new African poetry and drama in French, English, and, later, Portuguese, were already doing—probing the inner mysteries of indigenous mythology and symbolism. Only in this way could the enlightened African restore a sense of equilibrium in his people's culture.

D. T. Niane translated the Sundiata epic. Birago Diop began to grapple with the folktale, producing, as a result, French translations of *Les Contes d'Amadou Koumba.* Some were his own creations or adaptations in which the tales were retold in an idiom peculiar to him. Dadié does the same thing in his *Le Pagne noir* that Birago Diop undertook, and we are again indebted to Karen Hatch, a great admirer of Dadié, for most ably translating his stories.

Three of these tales—"The Mirror of Dearth"; the title story, "The Black Cloth"; and "The Man Who Wanted to Be King"—are Dadié's own creations. The use of *calvary* to symbolize the agony that attended little Aïwa's mistreatment at the hands of her stepmother is an obvious example of Dadié's modern idiom and sensibility. But here and in the other two stories he engineers an ending that has the cautionary effect of any folktale. The conscious interpretation and natural logic man

brings to the organic unity he *observes* in the universe ("The Man Who
Wanted to Be King")—in addition to simply *living* that unity—tells us
that we are reading a story told by a modern writer. The very fact that,
as we are told, the man distinguishes the oppressiveness of city life from
the freedom of nature represents a sensibility we would expect from
a modern story. The conscious poetry through which we perceive the
movement of the stream and the river is another indication of a con-
temporary poet imposing his own interpretation on the natural landscape. Yet other modern images are of an Eldorado and fairyland to
describe the riches of the city Ananzè finds himself in in "The Mirror
of Dearth."

The character that unifies all these tales in the volume is Ananzè the
Spider, so common throughout the folklore of West Africa and the West
Indies: cunning, plotting, resourceful, adventurous, ambitious, heroic,
and foolhardy. The mood that unifies them derives from the sense of
wonder in the folktale, the evil force that ensnares all humanity when
a sense of proportion is lost: when we despise other creatures as Ananzè
does the tortoise, when the reverence for life escapes us, when we try to
be rational about good fortune, seeking to probe the mystery behind it,
like the character who reveals the secret hiding place of the good boa.
The philosophical unity is created by the all-pervading humanism of
Africa; it is rooted in social relationships and in man as the measure of
his universe because he represents the whole range of being, from matter to God.

The fascinating thing about the internal machinery of any translation is that, in the most subtle sense of the word, it criticizes the original
and vice versa. And even in Hatch's English translation, twice removed
as it is from the original, we can experience that tension between an
indigenous sensibility and the foreign language being used to express it.

More and more African writers and scholars are undertaking research into the oral traditions in order to understand the poetic or to establish one, or for the joy of replaying the literary repertoire of a tradition. Interest in the oral tradition is growing, especially on university campuses where it would have been rare to find it before the mid-sixties. Other writers like Wole Soyinka, Chinua Achebe, Christopher Okigbo, J. P. Clark, and Okot p'Bitek introduce African mythology in their works as a functional element, to enlarge and enrich meaning. Folklore also lends their writing a distinctive resonance. Doubtless we shall see a rediscovery of more and more of our folklore. It is not yet popular reading, but all over, African radio is playing an increasingly significant role in broadcasting folktales. Let us hope *Le Pagne noir* in English will be followed by many more translations and adaptations and that it will inspire more research.

Es'kia Mphahlele
University of Witwatersrand
Johannesburg

TRANSLATOR'S PREFACE

Bernard Binlin Dadié, fiction writer, poet, dramatist, and the present minister of culture in the Ivory Coast, is well known in Africa and Europe but relatively unknown in the United States. Indeed, few of his works have appeared in English translation. *Climbié* (1956), his first long work of fiction, was translated and published in 1971; a translation of *La Ville où nul ne meurt* (1968) is forthcoming from Three Continents Press. Selected poems and tales have appeared occasionally, usually in anthologies of African literature.[1] This situation, however, is changing. The African Literature Association delivered a special tribute to Dadié at its meeting in the spring of 1986, and Three Continents Press will soon publish a book of critical essays entitled *Critical Perspectives on Bernard Binlin Dadié*, edited by Janis A. Mayes. For fifty years Dadié has been a major voice in African-French literature, and the African Literature Association's tribute to him incidentally coincided with the writer's seventieth birthday.

Along with Birago Diop (Senegal), in French-speaking Africa Dadié has been considered a leading writer of folktales and responsible in

1   See, for example, Austin Shelton, *The African Assertion* (Indianapolis and New York: Odyssey Press, 1968).

great measure for the worldwide dissemination of the African folktale. His poetry has been compared frequently (and favorably) to that of the renowned philosopher-poet and former president of the Republic of Senegal, Léopold Senghor; and the rich simplicity of his prose style has been acclaimed by many French critics and scholars, notably Charles Dobzynski and Armand Guibert. Guibert describes Dadié's style in this manner: "Sa prose dorée est d'un flux heureux, non sans une part de convention qui est inhérente au genre. . . ." And commenting upon *Climbié,* Dobzynski writes: "Tout le récit, très simple en lui-même, repose sur une multitude de notations d'une extraordinaire qualité évocatrice. . . . Il sait utiliser à merveille les ressources de cette langue française à laquelle Climbié rend hommage. . . ."[2] Two other tributes are also worth noting. Lilyan Kesteloot, in her famous study of the negritude movement, honors Dadié as a folklorist by saying: "Il faut rendre la palme qu'ils méritent à des auteurs comme Birago Diop [et] Bernard Dadié . . . qui, d'une manière parfois trop mal appréciée parce que très discrète, témoignent du patrimoine des ancêtres et en nourrissant l'art le plus authentique."[3] And David Diop, the Senegalese poet, has offered what surely must be the most laudatory statement on Dadié's poetry. Referring to *La Ronde des jours,* Dadié's second volume of verse, published by Seghers in 1956, he comments: "Notre

2   The statements by Guibert and Dobzynski appear in C. Quillateau, *Bernard Binlin Dadié: L'Homme et l'oeuvre* (Paris: Présence Africaine, 1967). Guibert: "His prose style is a golden happy flow, not without some of the conventionality that belongs to the genre" (p. 154). Dobzynski: "The entire *récit,* very simple in itself, rests upon a multitude of notations of an extraordinarily evocative quality. He knows how to perform wonders with the resources of the French language, to which Climbié pays hommage" (p. 159).

3   Lilyan Kesteloot, *Les Ecrivains noirs de langue française: Naissance d'une littérature* (Bruxelles: Université Libre de Bruxelles, 1963), p. 306. "One must award decorations of excellence to authors like Birago Diop and Bernard Dadié who, in a manner often too little appreciated because so discreet, bear witness to the legacy from their ancestors and from it cultivate the most authentic art."

continent doit à Bernard Dadié ses plus beaux accents d'amour et de fidélité. *La Ronde des jours,* autant que les légendes, est un hymne à la grandeur de l'Afrique, un acte de foi, le credo que tout Africain redira."[4] Confronted with the inevitable question, "Which genre do you prefer?" Dadié has always been evasive; in conversation, however, and only after some badgering, he once admitted that "La poésie est plus facile à écrire, car je la porte en moi."[5]

Born in Assinie (Ivory Coast) in 1916, Bernard Dadié belongs to the older generation of African-French writers that includes Birago Diop, Léopold Senghor, Ousmane Socé, Abdoulaye Sadji (all from Senegal), and Jean Malonga (from the Congo). Their entire childhood and early adult life were spent under unquestioned colonial rule. With the exception of Malonga, the older writers were either born and raised, or, as in the case of Dadié, educated in one or the other of the *vieilles communes* of Senegal: Gorée, Dakar, Rufisque, and Saint-Louis. Dadié attended the Ecole Normale William Ponty, in Gorée, and graduated with the Diplôme de Commis d'Administration. From 1936 to 1947 he was associated with the Institut Français d'Afrique Noire (in Dakar), and from 1947 to 1960 he served with the Ivory Coast Information Service. In 1960 he became the director of fine arts and research in his native country, leaving that post some time later to assume the ministerial post he now holds. It is significant that he, like so many other African-French writers, has wedded a life of literature to that of government service.

4 David Diop, as quoted by M. Battestini, S. Battestini, and Roger Mercier, in *Bernard Dadié: Ecrivain ivoirien* (Paris: Fernand Nathan, 1964), p. 62. "Our continent is indebted to Bernard Dadié for its most beautiful expressions of love and fidelity. *La Ronde des jours* is a hymn to the grandeur of Africa, an act of faith, the creed that every African will recite."

5 Interview with Dadié, Paris, November 24, 1968. "Poetry is easier to write, for I carry it within me."

The Black Cloth (1955) might best be viewed as an important testimony to what Dadié acknowledges is a very rich oral literature indeed, a "luxuriant folklore, whose roots strike deep into the earth," whose "values have proved their worth, and continue to mould the consciences of men in our villages."[6] Oral literature not only imparts knowledge; it also permits a cultural continuity in that, as tradition dictates, the knowledge is bequeathed by village elders—in the evening, around a fire—to those who, in due time, must pass it on. The literary evocation of oral tales, though perhaps more technically complex, nonetheless makes for an even stronger continuity. Today's audience is much broader and certainly more widespread; it can enjoy the dual roles of listener and reader. Thus, the text itself becomes as effective a teacher as the traditional storyteller (*griot*).

The Black Cloth is comprised of sixteen tales, ten of which center on the exploits of Kacou Ananzè Spider, the trickster so common in West African folktales. Like most folktales, those in this collection have familiar endings: something is explained, a lesson is learned, or a question (dilemma) is posed that needs to be resolved. In "The Sacred Cow," for example, we learn why the hyena looks the way she does today; in "Spider and His Son" we learn to beware of excessive curiosity; and in "The Hunter and the Boa," as well as in "The Man Who Wanted to Be King," we are given questions that, as either listeners or readers, we must contemplate and discuss—with ourselves, perhaps, but especially with others. Of the tale types represented in *The Black Cloth*, certainly the dilemma tales (known as *énigmes* in French) are the most intellectually stimulating. As William Bascom has well noted: "Even when they have . . . standard 'answers,' dilemma tales can evoke spirited discus-

---

6   "Folklore and Literature," a speech given by Bernard B. Dadié at the First International Congress of Africanists, Accra, 1962, reprinted in *The Proceedings of the First International Congress of Africanists, 1962*, ed. Lalage Bown and Michael Crowder (Evanston: Northwestern University Press, 1964), p. 207 (translated by C. L. Patterson).

sions. Like many other African folktales, their content is often didactic, but their special quality is that they train those who engage in these discussions in the skills of argumentation and debate and thus prepare them for participating effectively in the adjudication of disputes, both within the family or lineage and in formal courts of law."[7]

In "The Hunter and the Boa," a poor hunter snares a boa in one of his traps. The boa gives the man a choice: free the boa and be rich and powerful, or kill the boa and continue to be poor and miserable. The man releases the boa and journeys to the boa's village. There he is given two gourds, one of which, upon his return home, he is to throw to the ground. The hunter does so and is given a castle and all the wealth in the world. The second gourd he is to keep, for it provides him with the ability to understand all the world's languages. As the story unfolds, the man overhears a mangy dog forecasting the evils that will threaten him: famine, plague, fire, a flood, and, last, death. The first four catastrophes the man is able to weather because he can understand what the dog is saying and prepares for the events; the last, however, proves more difficult. The man learns that he will die at noon the same day unless he returns to the boa the gourd he was given. If he does this, of course, misery will visit him once more. We see him hovering over his wealth, brooding. At the end of the tale we hear: "The sun climbed higher; the shadows huddled beneath the trees; it was just about noontime, the fatal hour. The hunter kept hesitating; he paced back and forth, from the gourd to his wealth, from his wealth to the gourd. He still hesitated, and the sun kept climbing. It was almost noon. If you were in his place, what would you do?" The signal for deliberation has been given, the challenge posed.

The situation in "The Man Who Wanted to Be King" is even more

_____

7 William R. Bascom, *African Dilemma Tales* (The Hague and Paris: Mouton Publishers, 1975), p. 1.

intense because it hits closer to home and bristles with meaning. We are
given a man who wants the respect and power awarded a king. He approaches God and makes his desire known: "Gnamian, make me a
king." God tells him that a king must be able to render justice, true
justice, "the kind of justice that seeks out the truth and therefore acquits
or condemns without any other consideration." The man is sent home
to think over his decision. Four days later the man returns to God and
restates his desire. God imposes a task: "Go and take a good look at this
world; then come back and tell me what you saw." As he roams the
bush, the man witnesses arguments between the monkey and the lion,
between the elephant and the ant. In each case the disputes are brought
before the nobles of the bush, the mighty ones with "huge mustaches
and manes." And in each case, the smaller of the two animals is found
guilty. The situation at the end of the tale is more difficult, because at
this point men are pitted against chimpanzees; sheer size becomes a
crucial note here. In a complex series of events, man and chimpanzee
accuse each other of stealing the other's treasure. "The chimpanzees of
the city, or the men, and the men of the bush, or the chimpanzees,"
begin arguing. Again, the nobles of the bush enter the contest, for the
matter is brought before them. And faced with this dispute, they are
indeed uneasy. The man who would be king returns to God and recounts everything he has seen. God asks: "And what was the animals'
verdict?" The man replies: "I left before they had given it." The man is
sent back to find out what the verdict was and to return to God with it.
As soon as this is done, God will make the man a king. "The man who
had wanted to be a king . . . left and never came back. And the animals
have not yet given the verdict in the case between the men of the city
and the men of the bush. . . . Meanwhile, God is still waiting for the
man who wanted to be king. And he will be king, whoever brings the
animals' verdict to God. Would you like to be this happy man?"

In both of these dilemma tales, although the experiences given are of a rather narrow focus, the truths inherent are wide ranging and ageless. And it is here that the modern literary sensibility meets the oral tradition most poignantly.

Tales of orphans[8] are also popular in West African folklore, and Dadié's collection gives us two such tales: "The Pitcher" and the title story, "The Black Cloth." The reader familiar with European fairy tales will at once recognize certain common features: a wicked step-mother, an orphan-outcast who must journey into an unknown—often frightening—world, magic, miracles, and helpful assistants. The good characters are, of course, rewarded; the evil ones punished. And like all fairy tales, "The Pitcher" and "The Black Cloth" are, indeed, wonder-lands when it comes to possible interpretations.

"The Pitcher" introduces us right off to an orphan boy, Koffi, who has just broken a pitcher belonging to his stepmother. Angry, she sends him away to find one exactly like it. He is happy to go. "The farther away he got from the house—where everything he knew had been in the form of insult, forced labor, and punishment—the happier he felt." And the longer he journeys, the greater his sense of freedom, the more at ease he feels, the more his trust—of people and things—grows. He meets up first with a crocodile; then with a "strange creature who reeked and reeked of all the stenches in the world, a creature whose head was lost in the sky and whose feet were hidden in the ground"; next with a devil figure; and, finally, with a group of old women. To each he recounts his story; and each gives him a task to perform, with the promise that if the task is done he will see his mother who died giving him birth. Once Koffi has completed the tasks assigned to him by

8 For additional information on the orphan figure, see, for example, Susan Domo-witz, "The Orphan in Cameroon Folklore and Fiction," *Research in African Literatures* 12, no. 3 (1981): 350–58.

the old women—washing and combing and dressing each of them—he is given two gourds, one of which he throws at a given spot. He suddenly finds himself in the company of his mother who, after giving him three other gourds, says to him: "As you leave the village, throw this particular gourd. You'll immediately find yourself in your own village. The other gourds contain your fortune; and here is the pitcher you were looking for." Koffi does as he is told, but no one recognizes him in his own village, for so much time has passed. After giving the pitcher to his stepmother, he throws the other gourds, and they provide him with castles and riches and men and women and children to people the castles. He becomes king. The stepmother, her heart bloated with envy, sends her own son to "do as Koffi did. Get rich." The boy, however, refuses to perform the tasks asked of him by the creatures he meets (the same ones Koffi had encountered); and though he, too, is given gourds, they lead to far different results, the last of which is death and disappearance. The tale ends with an explanation: "And so it is that after the experiences of this woman, no one any longer mistreats an orphan in the country of black people."

The journey the orphan Koffi undertakes and the tasks he performs are all part of an initiation process. We watch young Koffi grow up. And the way in which he approaches the tasks—courageously, willingly— as well as the manner in which he actually does them—thoroughly and at great pain—prepares him, in the end, for his new role as king. The contact with his mother, moreover, leads to his reintegration into a society lost to him at birth. Clearly, then, alienation and integration are central themes in this story.

The orphan figure in "The Black Cloth" is a young girl named Aïwa, a beautiful young girl who always smiles, who always sings. Like Koffi, Aïwa, too, lost her mother at birth, and she also suffers insult and humiliation from her stepmother. The stepmother is jealous of the young girl's beauty, her gentleness and perennial good humor, and searches for a way to dull them all. Aïwa's journey—with all its attendant dreamscape qualities—begins when her stepmother tells her to "go and wash this black cloth." The young girl can go wherever she likes, but she must wash the cloth until it becomes as white as chalk. The first three waters that Aïwa tries refuse to even dampen the cloth; the fourth, however, does.[9] She plunges the cloth into a spring rising up from the earth in a clearing in front of her, and after several moons of washing, after a call—in song—to her mother, the mother appears, holding a white cloth. The mother exchanges the white cloth for the black one and then disappears. Aïwa takes the cloth to her stepmother, who recognizes it as one that was used to bury her husband's first wife. The tale ends: "But Aïwa just smiled. She always smiled. And she is still smiling the smile that one finds time and again on the lips of young girls."

In this story, a voice raised in song has reestablished the bond—natural as well as social—Aïwa lost at birth. We might ask, though, does the smile at the end mean that Aïwa realizes for the first time the kinship with her mother; or, rather, because she has always smiled, does it mean that what she felt and suspected earlier is, at the end, known? Whatever the case, a necessary kinship is recovered and restored.

The tone in both the dilemma tales and the orphan tales is serious, at times even melancholy. In the trickster tales, however, we find ourselves in quite another world: the wily and wonderful world of Kacou Ananzè Spider, the great leveler of gods, people, and things. (As Marie Tollerson, author of one of the latest studies on the structure of Dadié's

9   For a discussion of the symbolic elements in Aïwa's journey, see Wyatt MacGaffey's "The Black Loincloth and the Son of Nzambi Mpungu," in *Forms of Folklore in Africa: Narrative, Poetic, Gnomic, Dramatic*, ed. Bernth Lindfors (Austin: University of Texas Press, 1977), pp. 144–51.

tales, points out, it is significant that "whether Kacou Ananzè wins
or loses, the ability to challenge God is one he shares with no other
creature, and there is the struggle between them which is always re-
newed.")[10] Spider's protean nature has been the subject of much
scholarship in recent years;[11] he is, to be sure, shrewd, greedy, and
deceitful; and the sheer power of his imagination makes him at once
a master of games, words, and irony. Sometimes he comes out the
victor; at other times, however, he finds himself caught in his own web.
We are never certain of the outcome, and because we aren't, these tales
are especially appealing.

In "The Sacred Cow" we find Spider in the role of courtier, indeed,
God's favorite courtier. A famine exists and there is nothing more to
eat: "Nothing in the air; nothing in the bush; nothing in the water."
Everyone is growing thinner and thinner, except Kacou Ananzè. God is
not only curious as to why Kacou Ananzè is the only creature who
doesn't get thin, he is also bothered by the fact that his cow, "the most
beautiful cow in all creation" who he has taken such good care of, is
also getting thin. Her rations are increased, but she continues to waste
away. We learn that Spider is with the cow day in and day out, and we
also learn that he has shared, in secret, with the hyena (characterized in
so many West African folktales by an insatiable greed), the reason for
his rosy complexion. "His secret? Here it is. . . . Every night, Ananzè
would slip into the park through a crack; using a thousand clever ruses,
he would make his way into the sacred cow's stomach. There he would
eat his fill; then, from the same opening—he only had to tickle it a little
bit—he would emerge." One night, after Spider has repeatedly warned

10   Marie S. Tollerson, *Mythology and Cosmology in the Narratives of Bernard
Dadié and Birago Diop* (Washington, D.C.: Three Continents Press, 1984), p. 76.
11   See, for example, Robert D. Pelton, *The Trickster in West Africa: A Study of
Mythic Irony and Sacred Delight* (Berkeley: University of California Press, 1980).

Hyena not to touch the heart, the two are off to the park to enjoy a good meal. Once inside the cow's stomach, the hyena begins to gulp down everything, including, eventually, the heart itself. The cow collapses and dies, and the news of her death spreads quickly. Everyone comes to grieve, everyone, that is, except Kacou Ananzè and Hyena. An order is given to cut up the cow; and, in the process, the belly is thrown down, only to burst open and reveal a very angry Kacou Ananzè, who shouts: "What do you think you're doing? . . . Didn't you see me there? Didn't you see me looking for special herbs to cure the sacred cow?" Spider complains to God and is spared the brutal beatings the hyena is forced to endure. The hyena is beaten on the head and on the kidneys, "especially on the kidneys." And ever since then, we hear, "the hyena has looked the way she does today." So ends the tale.

Spider, however, is not so fortunate in the story "The Yam Field." He has worked steadily, month after month, to grow a beautiful field of yams, so beautiful, in fact, that anyone who happens by can't help feeling jealous. A thought keeps hounding him though, one that might add a "new and glorious chapter [to his] life," and provide yet a "new twist to his character": what if he ate all those yams by himself? After all, didn't he do all the work? Must he share all this with others? A scheme is adopted: "He was going to have to die. That was all there was to it . . . there was no other way." Kacou Ananzè and his family are busy working the field one day when, suddenly, he faints. Coulou, Spider's wife, is aware of her husband's tricky ways and urges her oldest son to keep an eye on him. One morning not long after his fainting spell, Kacou Ananzè announces to his family that he is going to die, that when this happens, he is to be buried in his field near the yams he has worked so hard to grow. Two days later he does die and is buried in that field. The funeral ceremonies drag on and on, and when they finally come to a close, Spider slips out of his tomb and stuffs himself with yams. This continues night after night. Coulou notices that the mounds of yams are shrinking and suspects her husband is to blame. She, too, has a scheme in mind.

One night, as Spider is making his way toward a mound of yams, he notices someone next to it. This someone grabs him and refuses to let go. As it turns out, the someone is nothing more than a scarecrow made of birdlime, but Kacou Ananzè is stuck fast. Day comes, and when he hears his children approaching, he pretends to be dead. "We've caught the thief!" they shout, "and he looks so much like Papa." To the question, "What shall we do with him?" Coulou replies, "We'll burn him." The flames bite and claw at him, but they also melt the birdlime. Kacou Ananzè pulls free, throws himself upon his wife and children, and drags them to a nearby stream. "Some of them were swept away; others floated on the surface. And ever since then, spiders have been floating on springs, streams, and rivers." In this tale, Spider escapes death only by chance and at a price. It is fortunate, however, he didn't die, for, as we hear at the end of "The Mirror of Dearth," "his adventures would have ended, and we men would have little to tell each other during the evening hours."

Spider is the same scheming creature in the other tales as he is in the ones summarized above. He is responsible for the "ugly black tongue" the sheep wears to this day; he is responsible also for the pig losing its fine, long trunk. But his cleverness does, at times, backfire. In the story "Spider's Hump," we learn that Kacou Ananzè becomes a hunchback because he refused to heed the advice of a group of dwarfs who warned him, time and again, not to sing their songs and dance their dances. In "The Dowry," Spider loses out in a contest to see who will be the husband of God's oldest daughter. The rules of the contest stipulate that the winner must, within a month's time, bring God a sample of everything that is eaten on earth. Kacou Ananzè fails because he forgets to bring some flies. In "Spider and the Tortoise," Spider tries to outwrestle a braggart tortoise, only to find himself defeated instead—and not just on one front, but on two. Spider had caught a squirrel in one of the traps he had set during a time of famine, and the squirrel, in exchange for his life, promised to take Kacou Ananzè to his own village, a marvelous land of plenty. When they arrive in the squirrel's village, Spider is fed and fed some more. All goes well until Tortoise begins to boast that no one can beat her in battle, but that if someone does, she will give the winner her handsome ram. A proud Kacou Ananzè, who wants the ram, but who wants even more to make sure his reputation remains intact, accepts the challenge. When the tortoise throws him into the air, he loses not only the battle but also the land of plenty he has been enjoying, for he suddenly finds himself back in his own village. At the end of the tale, we find Spider on the lookout for the squirrel's return.

Like many recent critics of folktales, Marie Tollerson also focuses on key themes at the heart of the tale. Of particular interest are the themes of water, death, strange lands, and trees. And each of these themes figures significantly in the tales comprising *The Black Cloth*.

Water is commonly seen as "not only the giver, sustainer, and restorer of life, but also disseminator of the 'word.' "[12] In "The Pitcher" and in the title story, for example, both Koffi and Aïwa encounter water. Aïwa, who has been told to make a black cloth white, attempts the task, first in a stream and subsequently in several springs. The last of the springs dampens the cloth and opens the way for the appearance of her dead mother who gives her daughter a white cloth. It is clear in this tale that water ushers in a rebirth, for, at the end of the tale, we must assume that Aïwa returns to her village not only "still smiling," but also to

12 Tollerson, *Mythology and Cosmology*, p. 16.

know a happy life. Koffi's experience is similar in broad outline, different in the particulars. In his journey to find a pitcher exactly like the one he broke, he meets up with a crocodile who takes him across a river and into a land of terrible noises and even more terrible creatures. In time, however, and after performing a number of specific tasks, he finds himself "in the company of his mother" who provides him with the wherewithal to know a happy life. Indeed, he returns to his village and becomes a king. Here, too, water is associated with a rebirth and proves a restorative.

In two other tales, however, water, though it ushers in a new life, has its regenerative powers spoiled by the central characters. In "Spider and His Son," for example, Spider-Son, having encountered a boa beside some "trickling springs," is taken by the boa to a marvelous land of gold and diamonds. There, Spider-Son becomes "the richest and most powerful king on earth." A condition exists, though: "Spider-Son must make sure that his benefactor is never seen by anyone." When Kacou Ananzè appears in the kingdom many years later, he discovers the boa Spider-Son has hidden, and the kingdom disappears. In "The Hunter and the Boa," a hunter snares a boa in a trap he has set along the banks of a river. The boa, in return for his life, makes it possible for the hunter to know wealth and, further, to understand all the languages of the world. But the hunter, now a wealthy ruler, misuses his powers in the hardships that come, saving himself and his family at the expense of others, and, in the end, finds himself confronted with a most difficult decision: to die or lose all his wealth. In these two tales, then, water is not only associated with life but also with death, symbolic or otherwise.

Water as perpetuator of the "word" is most clearly seen in "The Man Who Wanted to Be King" and "The Hunter and the Boa." In the former, Dadié describes a river and stream at odds with each other. "One day the river filed a complaint against the stream because the

stream kept singing a song that was similar to his, a song that he had
inherited from his ancestors." The description that follows, however,
shows clearly that the two waters are not alike. The river has a "monotonous voice"; it uproots branches and grasses and "drags them away
with him." The river is greedy and pitiless, with victims "always trailing
behind him." The stream, on the other hand, murmurs softly, "snuggles
up against a tree lying across her bed"; she serves as a mirror for
the earth's wonders; she "carries with her the laughter of young girls,
the songs of washerwomen, and the whisperings of bamboo trees and
reeds." She offers fresh, cool water to those who come to her burdened
with worry. The stream, however, is found guilty of imitating the river's
song and, as we hear, has "ever since then . . . taken her waters and her
song to the river." It is obvious here, as Tollerson has noted, that "the
activities of one are related to life; the activities of the other, to death."[13]
In the association of water to both life and death, though, this tale
shares in the symbolism of the others.

In "The Hunter and the Boa," as the boa is pleading with the hunter
to release him from the trap, Dadié postpones the hunter's decision to
free the snake and inserts the following description: "The waters flowed
by. Along the banks and in among the mangrove trees, they told a
thousand stories to the immovable land, a land that would never travel
to another region, but one that would always be crouching there, over
the water. . . . Stirring loose thousands of twigs along the banks, the
waters recounted their adventures to an attentive land, a land fascinated
by the exciting news that the indiscreet and forever-gossiping waters
had picked up while listening to the conversation between the hunter
and the boa just so they could repeat it farther on. . . ." This passage not
only prepares the way for the eventual joy—and subsequent sorrow—

13   Ibid., p. 14.

that will come to the hunter; it also furthers the idea of the perpetuation of the tale throughout the land, throughout time. We might add, though, that the passage also increases the suspense at this point in the plot.

With regard to the strange-land theme, it becomes quickly apparent that many of the regions that Dadié's characters pass through or journey to are, indeed, lands of the dead or of Death. And these "strange lands are," as Tollerson writes, "invariably far away from the village of the protagonist and those whom he knows and loves."[14] Sometimes they lie in lushly forested areas ("The Black Cloth," for example), sometimes in areas bereft of all stirrings of life ("Spider's Ox"), sometimes in areas at once frightening and magical ("The Pitcher"). In general, these strange lands are reminiscent of the forest worlds in many European tales, and here too they suggest a coming to terms with what one is. Usually, if the protagonists journey freely into those lands, confront their dangers head on, and successfully perform the tasks asked of them, they go on to lead happy, fulfilling lives; if, however—and this is frequently the case—they simply pass through such lands on their way to wealth, they are punished, for they have not earned their right to happiness.

Trees also appear in many of these stories, most notably in "The Mirror of Dearth" and "The Black Cloth." In "The Mirror of Dearth," Kacou Ananzè, who has known years of famine, becomes a fisherman and manages to hook a tiny sheat-fish. The sheat-fish says to Kacou Ananzè: "Put me back in the water, and you will be happy." In order to know this happiness, however, Kacou Ananzè must climb to the top of a silk-cotton tree and let himself fall from there. After some necessary persuasion, Kacou Ananzè does as asked, and finds himself "in the

14   Ibid., p. 38.

most marvelous . . . city in the world, the busiest trading center on earth." In that kingdom, he becomes prime minister. The tree functions here as a mother figure, as a "gateway to life." In "The Black Cloth," one of the springs Aïwa encounters is in the hollow of a tree trunk, another in a clearing surrounded by trees. "Since," as Tollerson informs us, "traditional African thought conceives the worlds of the living and of the dead to be joined by a tree,"[15] it comes as no surprise that soon the figure of her dead mother appears before Aïwa. Given such associations—of tree as mother, of tree as a link between the worlds of the living and the dead—we are, to be sure, also in the world of Near Eastern, Hellenic, and Nordic myth.

All the tales in *The Black Cloth* preserve many of the expressive features common to the oral storytelling tradition.[16] Several of the tales, for example, open with the familiar narrative phrase, "Il était une fois" ("The Black Cloth" and "The Man Who Wanted to Be King") or "Autrefois" ("L'Enfant Terrible" and "The Pig's Snout"), which may be translated "Once upon a time," "In the olden days," or, simply, "Once," depending on context and rhythm. Other stories, however, take the reader immediately into the plot; in "The Sacred Cow," for instance, a character—in this case Spider—has the first words: "And above all, Hyena, don't touch the heart." Still others begin with a statement of theme, where, then, it is the voice of an omniscient narrator that leads. "The Bat's Relations," for example, opens: "The bat was alone all day and all night, so alone, in fact, that the solitude weighed heavily on her." (The bat's efforts to alleviate this solitude become the focus of the tale.) This

15   Ibid., pp. 54, 58.
16   For a detailed review of the expressive features of folklore, see Dan Ben-Amos, "Introduction: Folklore in African Society," in Lindfors, *Forms of Folklore in Africa*, pp. 1–34.

type of opening is most often used, since it is the narrator who, through
his commentary, directs the tale and, therefore, what the reader learns
from it.[17]

The closings also vary, depending on the nature of the tale. Most of
the stories in this collection end, appropriately, with an explanatory
statement or with a question, which fulfills their didactic function. The
concluding line of "The Mirror of Dearth" (a story in which Spider
tempts Fate by looking in a forbidden mirror) is, however, one less
frequently encountered. Here, the narrator says, "And like all lies, it is
through you that mine will be thrown out to sea, to roam the world
over." These words not only signify the end of the tale but also assure its
perpetuation.

Songs and sounds are other features of the oral storytelling tradition, and Dadié makes careful use of both to enhance dramatic effects
that otherwise might be lost in the literary rendering of an oral form. In
"The Black Cloth" and "Mother Iguana's Funeral" the songs are crucial to the plot, and each is sung by a central character. As mentioned
earlier, Aïwa's song precedes the appearance of her mother, which, in
turn, permits the story's happy ending. The song Iguana-Son sings as he
and Spider journey to Iguana-Son's village to take part in the funeral
celebrations of his mother provokes Kacou Ananzè into playing a trick
on his friend, the results of which are the subject of the remainder of the
tale. We can imagine, of course, what dramatic effects might be in-
cluded in the oral performance of such songs; but these effects should
not be entirely lost to a reader with a good ear and a sympathetic
response to verbal art and nuance.

Of special interest is Dadié's transliteration of physical action into
sound. Such transliterations not only highlight the description of a par-

17   Eileen Julien, "Of Traditional Tales and Short Stories in African Literature,"
Présence Africaine, no. 125 (1983): 151.

ticular action, they also provide humor. In "Mother Iguana's Funeral," for example, once Iguana-Son and Spider reach the mother's village, Spider, who has given himself the name "Papa Stranger," is, as a "stranger" (guest), treated especially well. All the young girls bring him food and more food, which, for a while, he is able to enjoy all by himself. "He ate [it] all, without giving so much as a bite to Iguana-Son. He kept eating and clicking his tongue. He would suck on a bone for hours, and lick his fingers, *piô! piô!* and belch loudly, *gâhôwe!*" This continues. "How sweet it is!" says Spider, "I'm convinced, Iguana, that there are real cooks in this country, *piô! piô!* I think I'll come back here and take a wife, *gâhôwe!*" This same technique is found in "L'Enfant Terrible," where, at one point, we listen to a kettle chatter on a fire: "It whistled, raising the lid first on one side, and then on the other; it dribbled, and the froth fell into the fire, making a *chui!* . . . *chui!* sound like burning grease." In that story, too, we also hear the *clouk! clak! clouk! clak!* of the tortoise as she goes from one end of a village to the other.

Yet another stylistic feature Dadié borrows from the oral tradition, and the one most prevalent in all of the stories in *The Black Cloth*, is repetition, and not just of single words but of entire phrases. Often, the effects are rhythmical. In "The Pitcher," for example, when a frightened Koffi finds himself before a devil, we hear: "He would have liked to run from there. Yes, he must run; he must flee from these apparitions and return to the world of humans. He ran, and kept running, until he was out of breath. But the curious thing was, he had not budged at all from where he stood." A sense of frantic flight is achieved partly by rhythms of mental notation that break up into short fragments, partly by the recurring word "run." We are put immediately inside the mind of a child whose thoughts frantically come and go. At other times, the effect is both rhythmical and metaphorical. In the scene from "Spider and His

Son," where we find Kacou Ananzè anxious to escape a famine and yearning to reach his son's kingdom of beauty and splendor, Dadié writes, "[He] took the path straight ahead of him, walking in the direction he had thrown his son whom he had watched disappear in the distance. He kept walking, grinding his heels forward all the time. He encountered no one, not a single living soul. There was desert in front of him and desert behind him; there was burning sand on his right, a flaming ocean on his left, and a scorching sun overhead. He felt the heat waves all around him. . . ." Or it may be onomatopoetic, as in the lilting parallelism and repetition of consonants and assonantal vowels in the following passage from "Spider's Hump": "Donc dans la brousse étaient des nains, des nains danseurs, qui, toutes les nuits, venaient danser sous le fromager du village" ("There were dwarfs in the bush, dwarf-dancers who came every night to dance under the silk-cotton tree in the village").

Clearly, Dadié is a master of stylistic and scenic effects, and because the "meaning" of a story is often inseparable from them, a translator must struggle not to lose them in English.

The structure of Dadié's stories is, for the most part, episodic. This, too, they share with the oral story-telling tradition. Generally, and in a manner similar to that of a miniature epic, a situation is given at the onset (usually by an omniscient narrator), a character responds to it, and one response leads to another, rather like the links on a chain. Nothing is concluded until the very last line of the story, and what is concluded may be positive or negative, joyous or sad. (The final outcome of the dilemma tales, given their closing questions, must, of course, await completion.) Sometimes, as is the case in many of the famine tales, a hungry and miserable Kacou Ananzè becomes a well-fed and happy Kacou Ananzè, but something occurs—usually because of Spider's overwhelming pride or curiosity—to change the situation back to what it was in the beginning. At other times, and the orphan tales are an illustration of this, the story opens with a picture of hardship, and though the character is tested again and again (and often to the verge of despair), the hardship is eliminated and a better world reigns at the end. At still other times, notably in "Mother Iguana's Funeral," we have two characters who begin a journey together but who, eventually, are set apart. What happens to one does not happen to the other, and, in the end, the good character is rewarded and the evil one punished. Generally, however, we have a single "hero" or "heroine," and the structural pattern is neatly cyclical or linear.[18]

Two exceptions to this general structural pattern are worth noting: first, because they are examples of a more modern narrative style; and second, because we are permitted a look at a character from within rather than from without, as is the usual procedure. "The Sacred Cow" opens not with the distanced voice of a third person but with dialogue: Spider is warning Hyena not to touch the cow's heart. This is followed by the mental ruminations of Hyena, who is eager to play a trick on the master of tricks himself—Spider. "I may look stupid," she says, "but we'll see if I'm really stupid. . . . I'll be the one to eat that heart, *kpa*. I'll cut it out in a single bite, and *klouc!* I'll swallow it. . . . Tomorrow I'll be the one who walks away the winner; and after tomorrow, the entire world will know that I, Hyena, beat Kacou Ananzè at his own game." Only after we have the characters and plot line firmly in place does the narrator step in to tell us about God's special cow, Spider's privileged position with God, and the famine that exists on earth. "Spider's Hump," on the other hand, is entirely first-person narrative. Kacou Ananzè himself tells us the story of how he became hunchbacked. He

18 For a discussion of the most common structural types in the African narrative, see Dan Ben-Amos's review of Denise Paulme's research in this area, in "Introduction: Folklore in African Society," in Lindfors, *Forms of Folklore in Africa*, pp. 19–21.

begins, logically enough, by taking us into times past: "Back then," he says, "I was a handsome devil. There was no one like me in the whole world. . . . Women were dazzled and ran spellbound at my heels. . . . Many were the women who walked the distance of a moon, two moons, even twenty moons, just to see me. And when they saw me, they would forget to leave. . . . For that reason, I had a harem that was larger than ten, no, thirty, villages." He then takes us into the day, and into the particular circumstances, that left him as he is now, hunchbacked. All of those women who once flocked to him, he says, "now [hoot] at me instead of pitying me. Ah! if only they had been content to hoot at me! But no. They told the neighbor woman about it, and she told her neighbor. . . . By the end of the day, the whole village knew that I was hunchbacked." In this story, Kacou Ananzè becomes much more than a recognizable character type whose actions are embodied in his very name; he becomes, instead, a full-blown personage whose psychology is as fascinating as his verbal dexterity.

Although the stories in *The Black Cloth* owe much in their design to the expressive features and general structural patterns[19] of the oral story-telling tradition, in their precision—of dialogue as well as action—they are often reminiscent of the stories of Maupassant. Indeed, Dadié once remarked in an interview: "Toutefois il y a deux auteurs que sans faire des maîtres à penser, j'ai beaucoup lus: —Victor Hugo et Guy de Maupassant. De Guy de Maupassant j'appréciais les *Contes* pour leur structure, leur fond, leur forme."[20]

19   Aware of the taste of his Western readers, Dadié makes greater use of description (of scene, emotion, and mood) than is found in the oral counterparts to these literary tales. See Tollerson, *Mythology and Cosmology,* pp. 91–100.

20   Bernard Dadié, as quoted by C. Quillateau, in *Bernard Binlin Dadié,* p. 150. "Yet there are two writers whom, though they don't control what I write, I have often read: Victor Hugo and Guy de Maupassant. I have especially enjoyed Guy de Maupassant's stories because of their structure, their depth of meaning, and their form."

The position of a translator is, at best, a precarious one. There are no fixed rules to follow, and much more is required than merely reading the original work. Translators have the one very difficult and often impossible task of transposing a complete meaning from one language and milieu into another. With *The Black Cloth,* the problems are even greater than usual because Dadié's stories are re-creations, in French, of a traditional oral form; hence, the translator is twice removed from the original. Somehow, then, the translator must attain a style that not only gives the same effect as the original but also as that of Dadié's own elegant and cultivated style in French.

The commonest problems, page by page, were inherent, of course, in the French language itself. For example, the indefinite pronoun *on.* When Dadié is formal, the translator can probably use "one." At other times, African idiom is likely to require a "you," "we," or "they," a passive construction, or some other expedient. The tone of the last line of "The Black Cloth," for example, is that of a formal conclusion; and there, the indefinite "one" was used. The same problem arises with expressions like *voilà, voici,* and *c'est* or *ces.* Translating *ces* as "these" or "those" can sometimes make a real difference; and the various *-ici* and *-là* constructions in French can rarely be Englished directly. There is also the problem of capitalization with regard to the animals mentioned in the stories. The rule followed was that the name of an animal was capitalized when it was used as a proper noun—for instance, "It's a simple recommendation, Hyena my friend," but not when the name was used as a common noun: e.g., "The hyena's eyes glowed."

Certainly the most strenuous challenge for the translator of *The Black Cloth,* however, is Dadié's poetic prose, or, more precisely, the lyrical passages that often function as interludes between one action and another, between one response and another. French can get away with a series of verbs in a single sentence without losing the sense; English usually cannot, especially if the verbs are reflexives. For example, the sentence: "La fumée s'élève calmement dans le ciel, forme des ronds, se traîne, serpent sur le sol, se redresse, s'enroule sur elle-même, se déroule, puis se redresse à nouveau" ("The Yam Field"). The compromise was: "The smoke rose calmly in the air, forming circles as it crawled and meandered about over the ground, only to straighten up, curl, then uncurl itself, and straighten up again."

A full explication of stylistic problems would lead into endless particulars of symbolism, recurring key words and motifs, and nuances of point of view. Enough, perhaps, has been suggested to mark off several of the major trouble spots a translator encounters. With all this in mind, the deepest challenge for the translator remains, without question, a sympathetic humility before the work. *The Black Cloth* must be felt complexly. But then, so must a translation.

Karen C. Hatch
California State University,
Chico

THE BLACK CLOTH

THE MIRROR OF DEARTH

This was a mirror never to look in; if you did, psst! all good things would fly away, disappear, evaporate. To attempt to look you had to be Spider: brave, courageous, and fearless like Spider; curious but stupid like Spider. Yes, once again it was Kacou Ananzè who defied fate, but only after he had known dizzy spells and the blues, those attendant nightmares that hunger always drags behind her. This, after his stomach, bloated like a goat skin and as resonant as a well-warmed tom-tom, had permitted him to taste life's eternal joys, to contemplate the sullen pink of a sun tired of always chasing after an elusive moon; to swoon with joy because the evening breeze tickled the soles of his feet. That evening, the breeze had made herself so seductive, so captivating, had tickled the soles of his feet and blown on his neck and in his ears so much that he finally said to himself: "Why not look at myself in the mirror?"

Ah! I can hear you cry out: "One really must be an idiot to go that far!" I beg your pardon! And what about us? The rest of us who are always analyzing why we are happy, we who are always breaking open our playthings to see how they work—are we not in the same boat and just as curious? Besides, we must get it through our heads once and for all that one is not an idiot if he is called Kacou Ananzè. If he allows himself certain boldnesses, it is because he always has more than one trick in his head, more than one phrase on his tongue to help him out of a scrape. Ah no! You can't catch Kacou Ananzè like that! In order to get him, the elders would group themselves in ten, in twenty, even by the hundred . . . but despite the best of traps, he would always come out the victor. For when they thought they had him by the arm, they had hold of only one leg; and when they were convinced that they held him by the trunk of his body, there was only the trunk of a tree between their hands.

Kacou Ananzè! He delights in difficult situations; he delights in obstacles that enhance his powers, unshackle his intelligence, and spark ingenuity.

There was a famine in the village then. For three successive years, the rains had failed to keep their rendezvous. No longer did even one dark cloud lose its way in the sky. Starved, did the clouds die on route? In anger, the sun broiled everything; and the wind, in order to woo her, never stopped carting sand. The grasses no longer grew. Every day the dry earth would crackle, and then crackle some more. Not content to set fire to forests, the sun burned cottages. The trees, stripped bare, were pitiful to see. They resembled a woman whose head had been shaved, whose ornaments had been removed. The branches, the boughs, the twigs—one would have taken them for roots, tiny roots seeking to draw from the overheated air a nourishing sap they no longer found in the parched earth. The distress was general. One could not single out anyone in particular as the cause, because this time everyone suffered from the famine. In the beginning, one had tried to pick a quarrel with the monkey, who claimed to be the king of kings. And to state his claim, he would wander around, saying to all who came along: "The kings sit in chairs made from the trunk of the tree that I climb on to take care of my needs. Who then is king?"

To retaliate, because the monkey was talking about him without naming him, man would go about telling each and everyone: "It's the monkey, the monkey who brings us all this misfortune. Because he always climbs trees to take care of his needs, this is what he has brought down on us."

But to go on then and pick a quarrel with the monkey in times like this, a time when the monkey was jumping around on the branches, imploring God. Really now! The man could therefore find no one to listen to him. And once again, the animals made fun of him.

Every day the famine became more brutal. Despite their elaborate ceremonies, the fetishists were not the least bit successful in luring even the tiniest cloud to the country. Not even a wisp of fog. Famine gave her hand to death. She gave both hands, for so many died, so many.

Unable to escape the common plight, even Kacou Ananzè himself felt the pains of hunger: stomach cramps, dizzy spells, aches in his joints, buzzing in his ears, blurred vision. He felt weak all over. Every evening he wondered whether he would be able to get up the next day.

In order to keep going, he became a fisherman. He fished all the time. As to the art of fishing, no one could deny Ananzè's ability. He would throw out his line and pull in some sort of shellfish. But, as if to tease him, one of these thousand inhabitants of the water would nibble at the bait and drag the float to the bottom, only to let it go at the precise moment our fisherman was preparing to set the hook. Oh, those bandits, those bandits who refuse to let me take them! But he didn't get angry. What good would that have done? He had learned patience. The times demanded patience.

So Kacou Ananzè fished. Often he would spend the night on the bank, which was warm and free of mosquitoes. The water was receding onto its bed more and more each day, leaving everywhere a white sand, which, in the moonlight, seemed to be an immense shroud. It was settling back onto its bed to fight against the dryness, against the sun that heated everything. They were all gone, all of them: the cascades, the eddies, the whirlpools, the waterfalls crowned with foam! The trees, pushed far back on the banks by the receding water, were, only a short time ago, magnificent as they leaned over the shimmering waves, leisurely gazing at their necklaces of liana vines, their curled headdresses, and their jewellike clusters of fruit. Let's not even mention the reeds and the mangroves. They all had disappeared: everything was dead, burned to cinders. Having divorced themselves from the forest, the waters flowed sadly, without song, without even the slightest whisper that one could hear at the feet of the trees when the water was still a friend of the forest.

The waters from the lagoons and rivers, all those blue, white, and black waters carrying along with them promenading duckweed, water lilies, and tufts of reeds that turned round themselves, getting caught a moment here as if to give someone the news, leaving again suddenly, as if hurrying to reach the end of their voyage, all those waters with their flotillas and twigs gathered up here and there along the way; those waters, in their struggle to survive, fought painfully against the thirsty, white-hot sun. And they would doze, barely flowing. You should see them, you should see those waters getting lower every day! Were they hungry too?

Kacou Ananzè continued to fish. Stubbornly he fished along the banks of the trickling water. The great rivers that once frightened men both by their length and depth, those rivers with their tumultuous courses, devouring men and domestic animals, all those rivers were now forced to beat a retreat, to double up on themselves in order to resist; and, in so doing, they had become mere threads, puddles. Sometimes a swallow would lose her way in this torrid country and drink of this water. Burned all the way to the core, she would rise up again with cries of despair and shoot straight into the sky as if to go and tell God: "People are dying! You must save them!"

In truth, the earth was losing people. Some wandered around with flat bellies, bellies so flat that one wondered if they still housed any insides.

And still, Kacou Ananzè fished. For a week now, the float had not budged. It had not even winked—as we say in our country—to warn Ananzè: "Look out! Take care! A victim is on the end of the line." The float was mute.

"Ah, now I understand! I wasn't sitting in my usual place."

He sat down in his usual place. The float still did not budge.

"Wait! I wasn't sitting like this. But how was I sitting?"

"I had my feet spread apart like this, my head to the right, and the sack on the left."

He took that position, but the float still did not budge.

"How stupid I am! I wasn't holding the line this way! There . . . that's how I was holding it when I caught those shellfish."

He held his line as he had before. And the float still did not budge.

"What kind of spell has been cast on me? Am I going to die of hunger too? Me? Kacou Ananzè? Die of hunger? Never! Has Death really taken a fancy to me? Has hunger really weighed on me?" He threw his line out again. And still the float did not budge. Kacou Ananzè began to feel dizzy; he saw things, and he heard voices. He chattered on alone so that he himself could then impose silence, as though other people were doing the talking. . . .

"What? What's happening? I ask you, is this true? The float! The float! Look at it! It's moving! It's going under! Do you see it?"

Wide-eyed, Kacou Ananzè stared at the float, which was making tiny waves around itself as it moved.

"Do I pull up now? How should I go about this to make sure that I bring up some little shellfish?"

The float disappeared into the water. Our fisherman got up, placed one leg here, one leg there, like that, held his breath, closed his eyes, bent over, and *fihô!* brought in his line. Dangling at the end of it was a sheat-fish no bigger than the little finger of a newborn baby. Kacou Ananzè threw himself on it, took it in his two hands, and began to dance. There it was, the little sheat-fish, no bigger than the little finger of a newborn baby, whispering to him and trembling all over: "Have mercy on me, Papa Ananzè."

"What did you say?"

"Put me back in the water, and you will be happy."

"I know that old song. I sing it often to certain people, to those suckers I take in."

"Believe me, you will be happy."

"Enough of this twaddle. I won't be happy until I feel you in my belly."

"Listen to me."

"Go ahead, speak."

"You must climb that silk-cotton tree over there, all the way up to the twelfth branch."

"The shakiest one?"

"That very one. Let yourself fall down from there, and you will have all you desire."

"Why you're not stupid at all, are you, little sheat-fish no bigger than the little finger of a newborn baby? The very idea! Are you saying this to me? Me? The master of tricks? What Death couldn't do, you want to do? Never! Climb up that silk-cotton tree, let myself fall down and break my neck all because I took the advice of a child like you? Come on now, are you discounting my age and intelligence? All the experience I've had?"

"Trust me."

The voice was so imploring, the tone so frank, that Kacou Ananzè attempted the venture. In two leaps he was at the foot of the silk-cotton tree; he climbed up. One would have said that thousands of arms were pushing him, pulling him, toward the twelfth branch. Despite the enormous thorns, the trunk seemed to him smooth, even soft. Left on the bank white with light, the little sheat-fish nodded to him. And he was no longer little, but big, very big.

Ananzè closed his eyes and *floup*, jumped, but in such a way that his head wouldn't go first. A broken neck, and it's death; a broken arm or leg, and there's still life. Playing the skiff rocked by the waves, he had scarcely left the twelfth branch when he found himself in the most marvelous and opulent city in the world, the busiest trading center on earth. Men were coming and going, buying, exchanging, negotiating, bartering, speculating, transporting, unloading, delivering, and all without the least bristle of argument and discussion that ignores courtesy, the first rule in this fairy-tale land. And there were palaces and colored lights everywhere, giving the city a truly magical look by day as well as by night. No matter where you looked the view was forever changing. As for prosperity, I need hardly tell you about it. The bright and happy faces of the citizens alone would tell you what an Eldorado this was. Each one of them was a walking picture of health. It was a fabulous city, not only in size and activity, but also in population. Kacou Ananzè was astonished, and he whispered to himself: "That little sheat-fish didn't trick me after all."

He had fallen in a field where just about everything grew. And he ate and ate. And he grew fat. His cheeks were like that! with creases and rolls of fat all over. In the midst of this plenty, he lost all notion of time.

Someone surprised him in his quiet retreat one day, and he found himself being conducted to the queen of this prodigious city. Kacou Ananzè behaved himself so well that he became prime minister of the kingdom.

The queen had said to him, however: "You may do anything in my kingdom, anything in my palaces, but what you must never do is look at yourself in that mirror over there."

"Very well," replied Kacou Ananzè.

His misfortunes began that day. "In that they have given me everything, why shouldn't I look at myself in that mirror? This must be a magical mirror. Ah! this queen wants to see who's the smartest. What kind of behavior is that?"

And the mirror was over there, just like all the other mirrors.

"Well, if it's so plain to look at, it must mean that its powers are great."

The evening breeze never stopped tickling the soles of his feet, or blowing on his neck and in his ears. She caressed his whiskers and eyebrows. She so tickled the soles of his feet that . . . blew on his neck and in his ears so much that . . . Kacou Ananzè said to himself: "Why not look at myself in the mirror?"

And so he did. But he immediately found himself once again at the edge of the river with the burning banks, the line in his hand, the float immobile.

And he was hungry! so hungry! He threw out his line, and threw it out again. The float went under. Ananzè brought in the line. Hanging from the hook was a tiny sheat-fish no bigger than the little finger of a newborn baby. Our fisherman was very happy and carefully unhooked him. The sheat-fish said nothing.

"Well! Well! Here's my friend the sheat-fish. How are you?"

". . ."

"Don't you recognize me? Ah! yes, that's it . . . you like to do good in secret. . . . Just the same, I'll prove to you that you know me."

". . ."

"But it's me, Spider, Kacou Ananzè . . . Spider, from the other day!

Don't you remember our last meeting? It was a morning like this one. . . . I had taken you out of the river, and you said to me. . . . How did you say it? Ah! . . . yes . . . 'Have mercy on me. . . . Trust me. . . . You will be happy. . . . Listen, you will have the good fortune. . . .' "

". . ."

"Must I broil you?"

"If you want."

"Come on now, what do you take me for? Would I broil my friend? That, I would never do! Do you want me to put you back in the water?"

"If you want to!"

"Are you going to tell me to climb up on the twelfth branch of that silk-cotton tree again? The last time, at your urging, I scrambled up to that twelfth branch, and from there, *floup!* I jumped. . . . Oh! how frightened I was at the beginning . . . but you, there on the bank, you nodded at me, you encouraged me in this feat. . . . Do you want us to start all over again?"

"If you want!"

"If I want! But that is what I want. Wait! Look, I'm going to climb up. I'm climbing."

It was truly painful climbing too. The huge thorns were like barbed wire and thwarted him at every step. Kacou Ananzè bled. Nevertheless, he reached the twelfth branch and played, once again, the skiff balanced by the swells. But feeling dizzy, Kacou Ananzè went crashing to the ground.

Fortunately, he did not die; his adventures would have ended, and we men would have little to tell each other during the evening hours. . . .

And like all lies, it is through you that mine will be thrown out to sea, to roam the world over. . . .

THE BLACK CLOTH

Once upon a time there was a young girl who had lost her mother. She had lost her on the very day she came into the world.

Labor had lasted for a week. Several older women had kept running over. But the labor pains persisted.

The first cry of the baby girl coincided with the last sigh of the mother.

The husband gave his wife a splendid funeral. Time passed, and the husband remarried. Little Aïwa's calvary began on that day. There were no deprivations or insults that she did not suffer; no hard labor that she did not do! And yet she would smile all the time. Her smile irritated the stepmother who kept harassing her with snide remarks.

Little Aïwa was beautiful, truly beautiful, more beautiful than all the other girls in the village. And this too irritated the stepmother, who envied this glorious, captivating beauty.

The more she increased the insults, the humiliations, the forced labors, and the deprivations, the more Aïwa smiled, the more beautiful she became, the more she sang—and this little orphan girl sang wonderfully. But she was beaten because of her good humor, beaten because she was the first to rise and the last to go to bed. She would awaken

before the roosters and go to bed only after the dogs themselves had
gone to sleep.

The stepmother no longer knew just what to do to get the better of
this young girl. She looked to find a way: in the morning when she
awakened, at noon when she ate, in the evening when she dozed. And
these thoughts hurled beastlike sparks from her eyes. She searched for
a way to end the young girl's smiling, to stop her singing, to dull her
radiant beauty.

She searched for a way with such perseverance and such eagerness
that, one morning, as she was leaving the hut, she said to the little
orphan girl: "Wait up! go and wash this black cloth. Go wherever you
like, but wash it so that it turns as white as chalk."

Aïwa picked up the black cloth that the stepmother had thrown at
her feet and smiled. For her, the smile took the place of complaining, of
moaning and crying, of sobbing.

And this magnificent smile which charmed everyone for miles
around put fire in the heart of the stepmother. It sowed coals in the heart
of the stepmother. And with all her claws showing, she fell on the little
orphan girl who kept smiling.

Finally, Aïwa grabbed the piece of black linen and left. After having
walked for a moon, she arrived at the edge of a stream. She immersed
the cloth in the water. It was not the least bit wet. And the water flowed
along calmly, little fish and water lilies playing on its bed. On the banks,
the frogs swelled their voices as if to frighten the little orphan girl who
smiled. Aïwa once again immersed the cloth in the water, but the water
refused to dampen it. She then resumed her journey, singing:

> "Mother, if you could see me on the road,
>   Aïwa-o! Aïwa!
> On the road that leads to the river,
>   Aïwa-o! Aïwa!

The black cloth must become white,
And the stream refuses to dampen it.
    Aïwa-o! Aïwa!
The water slips by like the day,
The water slips by like happiness,
O Mother, if you could see me on the road,
    Aïwa-o! Aïwa!"

She kept going. She walked for six more moons. Lying across the road in front of her was a huge silk-cotton tree; and in a hollow of the trunk there was some water, completely yellow but very clear water, water that slept beneath the breeze; and all around this water enormous ants with huge pincers stood guard. And these ants were talking to each other. And they were going and coming and crossing in front of each other, dispensing orders. Perched atop the main branch, which pointed a pale, dead finger toward the sky, was a huge vulture, whose wings obscured the sun for leagues and leagues. Its eyes threw out flames, like flashes of lightning; and its talons, like powerful aerial roots, dragged the ground. And it had one of those horrible beaks!

The little orphan girl immersed her black linen in this yellow and limpid water, but the water refused to dampen it.

"Mother, if you could see me on the road,
    Aïwa-o! Aïwa!
The road to the spring that will dampen the black cloth
    Aïwa-o! Aïwa!
The black cloth which the water from the silk-cotton tree refuses
    to dampen
    Aïwa-o! Aïwa!"

And she continued on her way, smiling always.
She walked for moons and moons, for so many moons that no one

remembers the exact number any longer. She walked by day and by night, never stopping to rest, nourishing herself on fruits gathered alongside the road, drinking the dew deposited on the leaves.

She reached a village of chimpanzees and told them her story. The chimpanzees thumped their chests with their two hands, as a sign of indignation, but after a while they gave her permission to wash the black cloth in the spring that flowed through the village. But even the water from this spring—it too—refused to dampen the black cloth.

So the little orphan girl resumed her journey. She was now in a truly strange place. The road before her opened up only to close again behind her. Everything talked: the trees, the birds, the insects, the earth, both the dead leaves and the dry leaves, the liana vines, and the fruit. And yet, there was no trace of a human being. She was knocked about and hollered at, little Aïwa was, as she walked and walked, only to realize that she had not budged since she had started walking. And then, all of a sudden, as if pushed along by some wonderful power, she leaped over distance upon distance, and found herself plunging still deeper into the forest where an agonizing silence reigned.

There was a clearing in front of her and, at the foot of a banana tree, a spring rose up out of the earth. She knelt down, smiling. The water quivered. And it was so clear that it reflected the sky, the clouds, and the trees.

Aïwa took some of this water and threw it onto the black cloth. The cloth became wet. Kneeling at the edge of the spring, she spent two moons washing the cloth, but it still remained black. She would look at her hands that were covered with blisters and then go back to work again.

> "Mother, come and see me!
> Aïwa-o! Aïwa!
> Come and see me at the edge of the spring,

Aïwa-o! Aïwa!
The black cloth must become as white as chalk,
Aïwa-o! Aïwa!
Come and see my hands, come and see your daughter!
Aïwa-o! Aïwa!

She had scarcely finished singing when there stood her mother holding a white cloth, a cloth whiter than chalk. She took the black cloth and, without saying a word, melted into the air.

When the stepmother saw the white cloth, she was stupefied; her eyes grew big. She shook, not from anger this time, but from fear; for she recognized one of the white cloths that was used to bury her husband's first wife.

But Aïwa just smiled. She always smiled.

And she is still smiling the smile that one finds time and again on the lips of young girls.

THE PITCHER

"So! You've broken my pitcher! I knew you would. It just took you longer than I thought. Well, you know what you must do. . . . I must have a pitcher exactly like the one you've just shattered. Go and find one for me where you will, but under no circumstances are you to set foot in this house again without my pitcher."

With the fragments of the pitcher at his feet, the petrified Koffi stared at his stepmother.

"How much I'd like to brain you! Haven't you stared at me long enough? What are you waiting for? Go where you will . . . but my pitcher, I must have it . . . do you hear? Do you understand?"

So Koffi left. He was happy to go, happy to leave this house where, ever since he had lost his mother, he had never found a moment's rest, a moment's joy.

The farther away he got from the house—where everything he knew had been in the form of insult, forced labor, and punishment—the happier he felt. He was rediscovering a taste for life. He met up with some men and chatted with them; with some animals, and he joked with them. No more insults, no more threats, just laughter, affection, and understanding. And when he told them all his story, he felt commiseration and pity in their voices and in their looks. And everyone said to him: "You could live there, in that hell, with such a devil at your heels all the time?"

Koffi continued on. And the strange thing was that the longer he kept going, the more life seemed beautiful to him. How truly small and limited his horizon had been! . . . In front of him was the world—space! He gazed at this world through eyes that now were dry. The tears that had distorted everything were gone; so were his feelings of loneliness, deprivation, wretchedness, and continual fear.

Koffi still walked on; and the farther on he went, the more his trust in people grew. He was at ease as he breathed in the healthy air, and he sang with such a marvelous voice that the leaves danced on their branches while the branches swayed on the trees. And the trees, drunk from the melody in the blowing wind, entwined their headdresses which were dotted with bright-colored butterflies busy flirting with some bees who were trying to rest.

And still Koffi kept going, Koffi who had never known his mother's slightest caress, or even her faintest smile, and about whom he remembered nothing. She had closed her eyes when Koffi had opened his on the world. It was said that in this vast universe, there had not been enough flame, enough light, to shine at the same time in the eyes of both Koffi and his mother, and that it was up to the mother to transmit her own flame to her son. Her life had died out as the child's was illuminated. . . .

One evening he arrived at the bank of a river which was so big that the other bank seemed to blend into the horizon. And there was a crocodile in this water who was as gigantic as a mountain. Gulls flew overhead, and the river was like a smooth carpet drawn along by an invisible hand. Small waves came up to die on the banks without leaving any lacy foam, like a single piece of velvet that is being unfolded. In the thick woods, the temple cocks sang out the hour of rest.

The crocodile stared at Koffi with his flame-colored eyes full blazing. Round about him tadpoles were chasing each other. Tufts of grass, like travelers looking for asylum in a village at evening, latched onto some reeds whose heads were in the water and confided who knows what secrets. A kingfisher, on the watch, scarcely beat his wings. The small fry navigated in squadrons; shellfish dragged along their thick, spiny bodies and staggered about as though they were burdened with a cross. A spider sat poised on a leaf and floated with the current. And always there were the shellfish who kept falling down and picking themselves up again, leaving little grooves and wakes on the sand.

The crocodile opened his mouth which was planted with huge, sharp-pointed teeth, teeth as large as silk-cotton trees, blackened and chipped from having eaten good things, and said to him:

"Who showed you the way to my house, little one? Ever since the world has been a world, no human being has ever come to these parts. What are you looking for? Do you want to be eaten up?"

"I'm only a little orphan boy. If you must eat me, listen first to my story."

And Koffi told the crocodile his whole story, from the death of his mother up to the day he had broken the pitcher.

Moved with pity, the crocodile shed tears—real tears they were—and answered him:

"I've just been taking a bath. If you scrub my back—you'll not only see your mother, but you'll also have a pitcher exactly like the one you broke."

And without a moment's hesitation, Koffi jauntily grabbed the sponge, stepped into the water, climbed up onto the crocodile, and began to scrub the gnarled and fissured back with its jagged edges as keen as the sharpest machete, spines as tapered as needles, and patches of scales where the soap would not lather. Koffi scrubbed and scrubbed the back; blood flowed from his gashed fingers and torn hands, reddening the water. But he didn't shed one single tear. After this laborious washing, the crocodile said to him: "Climb back up on my back."

The child climbed up, and they left.

One morning they found themselves in front of a door, a tiny little door and a very dirty one. The crocodile said: "Touch there."

Hardly had Koffi's finger brushed the door when a terrible noise was heard, a noise like the growling of a thousand thunderclaps and a thousand mountains tumbling down all at the same time. And what do you think he saw in front of him? A strange creature who reeked and reeked of all the stenches in the world, a creature whose head was lost in the sky and whose feet were hidden in the ground. And when he walked, he would rip open both the earth and the sky.

"Where do you come from, little reckless one? Who led you here? What do you want?"

The crocodile had disappeared the moment the monster showed himself. Koffi was alone; his heart wanted to break through his ribs and run off. But the ribs held firm, even though the heart had hurled itself against them. Koffi kept quiet, dumb with fright.

"What do you want?"

Koffi recovered his wits and told him his entire story, from the death of his mother up to the moment when he had seen the crocodile.

"Comb my hair!" exploded this strange creature.

And Koffi started combing. The slightest strand of hair that fell made the earth tremble. One could see the trees lurch forward and lean against each other, their headdresses becoming entangled, then go crashing down; the mountains swayed. And the hair stank: a suffocating, unbreathable odor.

But Koffi continued to comb him. He never knew just how long that took. But when he was through, the strange creature whispered to him: "Turn around."

Koffi turned around.

"Look at me."

Koffi trembled. Before him stood a devil more frightening than the crocodile and the strange creature. He would have liked to retrace his steps, to be far away from these parts. He would have liked to run from there. Yes, he must run; he must flee from these apparitions and return to the world of humans. He ran, and kept running, until he was out of breath. But the curious thing was, he had not budged at all from where he stood. He wanted to cry out. He screamed and screamed with all his might. But no sound whatsoever came out of his wide-open mouth. And in a voice more thunderous even than that of the crocodile or the strange creature, the devil over there yelled at him: "Where do you come from? Who led you to this country where no man has ever set foot? What are you looking for to have come all this way to me?"

And once again, Koffi told his story, from the death of his mother up to the encounter with the monster whose head was lost in the clouds and whose feet lay hidden in the ground.

The devil then led him to a sinister-looking place. The darkness there was opaque, dense, and palpable. It offered resistance as they passed through. And there inside were beings talking, laughing, singing, and dancing. How long had they been walking? Koffi could never tell. But suddenly they were in the light, and at the top of a very high mountain.

The devil turned toward Koffi and asked: "What did you see in the place we just went through?"

"Nothing."

"Let yourself fall off this mountain."

A mist spread out far and wide, from the foot of the mountain to as far as the eye could see. No trees could be seen; no noises could be heard. And the sun was blazing down upon this mist.

Koffi let himself fall off the mountain, at the bottom of which he once again found the devil, who handed him two keys, bidding: "Continue on."

"But what about these keys?"

"I will explain. On your way you will find two doors, one to the right, the other to the left. Open the one on the right; be very careful not to touch the one on the left."

So Koffi took his leave. He arrived at the two doors and opened the one on the right. It was the door to the village of old women.

"Where do you come from, little one, and where are you going?"

Koffi once again told his story in detail. Everyone wanted to hear it in order to be able to retell it in turn. And he told the same story to each one, with not a word more or less.

"You want to go and see your mother so that you can have a pitcher just like the one you broke?"

"Yes."

"Before you go, you must comb our hair, clean our fingernails and toenails, fetch water for us, and wash and dress us all."

It was a world of its own, this village of old, gray, broken-down women, all tottering on their canes as they came and went. Whenever they would get up, you could hear their joints cry out. Some of them could no longer even straighten up, and they would move around with their right hand holding the cane on which they leaned, their left hand resting on their hips as if to stifle the cries.

Yet Koffi submitted to this new test willingly and with a smile. He came and he went, telling funny stories to all the old women who slapped themselves on their thighs and held their stomachs as they laughed.

The oldest of the women was very happy that the last test had been met. She gave Koffi two gourds and told him when and where to throw the first.

Koffi started out again. At the chosen spot, he threw the first gourd. Scarcely had it touched the ground when Koffi found himself in the company of his mother who, in exchange for the key and the second gourd, gave him three other gourds, saying: "As you leave the village, throw this particular gourd. You'll immediately find yourself in your own village. The other gourds contain your fortune; and here is the pitcher you were looking for."

Joyfully, Koffi carried off his gourds and the pitcher. He finally had the pitcher! And at what pain! what suffering! His experiences with the crocodile, the strange creature, the devil, the old women—they all would have seemed a terrible dream to him were it not for the scars still on his hands, were he not holding the pitcher and the gourds!

When he threw the first gourd his mother had given him, he found himself once again in his own village. But he had grown so old that no one recognized him anymore. They had already forgotten that one day, years ago, a certain little orphan boy had left the village in search of a pitcher, the very same pitcher that he was returning with. So many years had passed since then that the old people visibly strained to remember him. They questioned the smoke from their pipes, their white beards, their long streams of saliva . . . they scratched their heads, rummaging through stacks and stacks of memories.

Koffi handed the pitcher over to his parents. He then broke the second gourd, and castles sprang up everywhere. The people saw them rise up from the earth, one after the other, golden castles that could not be looked at under a rising sun. And they kept coming, more and more of them, for as far as the eye could see. The sun would emerge from them, only to go back in at night, to sleep. From the third gourd came men and riches, women and children. All that, to people the castles.

Koffi became king.

The stepmother could not tolerate that. She wanted an identical fate for her own children—no, an even more glorious fate. It became an obsession with her. She lost sleep and appetite over it. The envy in her heart had grown roots as large as those of a silk-cotton tree and as thick and deep as those of a mahogany tree; it was entangled in webs more dark and deceitful than those of a spider. And as soon as the sun would come up, she would pray that it would melt all of the golden castles. But, as if to taunt her, the sun shone on calmly; and the rays from the gleaming castles pierced her heart like arrows. Every day her heart would swell up, bloated with envy.

One morning she walked out of her house even before washing her face and *pan! pan! pan!* jumped on her oldest son.

"You little scamp! Look over there! All that, and you just sleep and eat and laugh! Look at those castles. You must get some. We've got to have them. And more than that. Our castles must be made of diamonds and cover the entire earth. Go! do as Koffi did. Get rich."

And shoving her son by the nape of his neck, she started him on his way.

And, as if pushed on by the wind, the oldest son left.

Seeing the crocodile on the way to the river, he cried out: "Oh my! what a horrible crocodile. My God! what a monster!"

"Who sent you, little one?"

"My mother."

"And where are you going in such a hurry?"

"I'm off to become rich and powerful, like Koffi."

"Ah, but he was very kind, Koffi was."

"Not any more than I am."

"Wash my back, and I'll help you."

"Wash your back? Me? A crocodile's back? With all those spines and needles and all that filth gathered from who knows where?"

"Wash my back."

"My mother didn't tell me to go and wash backs, but to go and look for money and power. As for backs to wash, there are some back home in the village, and very smooth backs too, the backs of men, not crocodiles. I order you to help me across this river."

And the crocodile said to him in all sweetness: "Climb up on my back, and we'll go. Over there, where you're going, you'll find what you'll find."

"What will I find?"

"What you're looking for. Climb up."

And the child climbed up. The crocodile deposited him in front of the door that, on opening, revealed the monster whose head touched the sky and whose feet plunged deep into the ground. Instantly the child exclaimed: "What's that? What am I seeing? Hey, you, what's your name? But where's your head? And your feet? And what kind of hair is that? Is it made of branches? You don't have lice, do you?"

"Cut my hair."

"So you think I came here to cut your hair, do you? If it had been for that, I'd have stayed in the village. I came to make a fortune, I did, and to become as powerful as Koffi."

"Continue on your way. You'll find what you'll find."

"What will I find?"

"What you are looking for."

And the strange creature led him to the devil's house, and the devil, in turn, showed him to the top of the mountain; and from the mountain sent him to the village of old women whose joints, every time they moved, made noises like gigantic cranes that had never been greased. And they came and went, one hand on their hips, the other holding a cane on which they leaned. And their hair was as white as cotton. And not a single tooth was left in their mouths.

"What a place! What are you waiting to die for, you old ones? I'll bet you're all sorcerers. It's you who kill the young people whose beauty you envy, whose youth. . . . Don't look at me like that, you pack of witches. . . . Me, you won't kill. . . . Not a single one of you will suck the marrow of my bones. . . ."

But all of the old women ran up to him, clamoring: "Cut our hair! clean our fingernails, our toenails; wash us, fetch water for us, and we'll help you."

"Me help you? I was just going to ask you the same thing. But I can help you as well, help you die."

And the oldest of the old women handed him four gourds, saying: "You'll see what you'll see. As soon as you throw this first gourd on the ground, you'll find yourself at home again. As for the other three gourds, break them, and you'll see what you'll see."

The child threw the first gourd and found himself back in his own home, in the company of his mother, who was ecstatic.

"That didn't take you long! And here you bring us wealth and power! Give me those gourds. Where shall we put them? But why save them? It's better to break them right away . . . yes, immediately, so that our castles will rise up next to those. . . . Thank you, my son! . . . Come, so that I can press you against my heart, for you have freed it of an enormous weight. Just think, if I hadn't pushed you out by the nape of the neck that morning, you'd still be here looking at the sun rise up from those castles which ours will soon eclipse. . . . How should we hold the gourds? Yes, let's hold them like that, and may the whole world be covered with castles, our castles! . . . How my heart beats! Listen to it. Look how my hand is shaking! Look, my son! Look at all of those golden castles. Any minute now, and they'll all be swept away. A fortune we have in this gourd! And power in the other one. Thank you, my son. I can breathe now. I can live. I can look at the sun and hold my head up. From now on may the sun shine bright throughout the world and sow its beams from our castles."

And then, with all her might, the woman threw the first gourd to the ground. Lions, tigers, and jackals—all the wild beasts of the world—suddenly appeared. In order to ward off this fate, she broke the second gourd. Flames shot forth from everywhere, from the sky, from the earth and the wind, from the rocks and the mountains. Everything around them was in flames. The wild beasts chased after them. They ran and ran. The flames were faster, however, and cut off their retreat from all sides, encircling them, rising higher and higher like an immense red tower.

The third gourd was thrown. All of a sudden the earth opened up; it swallowed them and closed back over again. But shining with all their might in the setting sun were Koffi's castles.

And so it is that after the experiences of this woman, no one any longer mistreats an orphan in the country of black people.

SPIDER'S HUMP

Su-boum! Su-boum-ka!
Su-boum! Boum! Su-boum-ka!

And the tom-tom would move on through the forest, following the winding trail that had been made smooth by men and rainwater.

Years and years have passed since then. But the rhythm lingers yet in my ears. And I would still be able to manage a few steps to its soul-stirring beat.

Do you hear the tom-tom filling the bush and the village with its high-pitched notes so warm, so muted, so poignant? Do you hear it climbing up from the small valleys, descending from the mountains, peeking through the cloudbreaks, rising up even as high as the tinkling sound of the dwarfs?

You would think that this wailing tom-tom did not want to leave, for it rumbled so, and cried, and howled! It would be still a moment, then return again, faster than the wind that carried it.

Take care not to dance, however.

And take care not to repeat with the bewitching tom-tom its:

Su-boum! Su-boum-ka!
Su-boum-boum! Su-boum-ka!

For when I sang this song and danced that dance of the dwarfs, I became hunchbacked, I, Kacou Ananzè.

Back then I was a handsome devil. There was no one like me in the whole world. Not in the world of men, nor in the world of animals. Nowhere could you find a creature so handsome, so charming as I. Women were dazzled and ran spellbound at my heels. There was no way to break open this human cluster. Many were the women who walked the distance of a moon, two moons, even twenty moons, just to see me. And when they saw me, they would forget to leave. And when they were ready to give birth, every one of them was determined to name her baby Kacou Ananzè, as if the name Kacou Ananzè could beautify a monstrous ugliness and correct hideous features, as if it could bestow a bit of intelligence, smooth over any boorishness, and even make invalids well again. At the slightest fuss, these women would proclaim to their husbands, and loudly so in their ears: "Ah! If only I had a husband like Kacou Ananzè!"

"Go on then, marry him!"

And the women would snatch up the answer and come to my house. For that reason, I had a harem that was larger than ten, no, thirty villages.

Even the king's wives abandoned him to come to me. I welcomed them with open arms. Noblemen's wives had also joined the harem.

Whenever someone called me, I would answer with my motto: "A woman is like a jewel that must never be left to tarnish." Hearing that, the women would come rushing up to me. By now, all the women of the world would have joined my harem if . . . if it had not been for that tom-tom whose rhythm the dwarfs still let reverberate in my ears:

Su-boum! Su-boum-ka!
Su-boum! Su-boum-ka!

And furthermore, I must tell you that everything I did was done with a certain art. I talked well, and I danced well; I played the same way and dressed with inimitable style. There was nothing I could not do, and skillfully too. I had that in my blood. And because I could trick the others so well that I never got caught in their traps, I also gained the reputation of being a sorcerer, which made me grow even taller in the eyes of everyone, especially the women!

Women, as you know, have this weakness for mystery which they cultivate with consummate skill. There is always a slight veiling about their words and acts; a pinch of shadow in their laughter so that you must uncover the meaning behind it; an ounce of shadow in their expression so that they can maintain a certain eloquence; a morsel of shadow in their rendezvous so that you stew there, weaken, and end up at their feet.

Yes, I knew women, I did. I tell you that I had a harem equal to two hundred villages!

Everyone spoke only of me. I could not even begin to tell you how far my fame had spread. To give you an idea, let it suffice to say that the rain, the wind, and the water—everything in nature—spoke only of me, Kacou Ananzè, Spider.

But having great fame and unlimited fields, women by the hundreds, and children by the thousands by no means implied a change in habits. As for me, I liked to sing and dance. To sing more than the birds did; to dance more than the dwarfs liked to dance.

Su-boum! Su-boum-ka!
Su-boum-boum! Su-boum-ka!

All the same, take care not to beat out the rhythm with your feet or your fingers, for you never know—as is always the case in this world—where the dwarfs are going to be. . . . if you know what I mean.

Well, there were dwarfs in the bush, dwarf-dancers who came every night to dance under the silk-cotton tree in the village. And they sang beautifully, they truly did! Every night, year after year, they sang and they danced. . . . And it was prohibited for anyone who was not a dwarf to sing their songs and dance their dances. Everyone in the villages knew that. As soon as the children began to walk and talk, their mothers' first advice to them would always be: "Never sing the dwarfs' song. And never dance the dwarfs' dance; for if you do, beware of the hump!"

But as for me, Kacou Ananzè, every night, as soon as I heard the song and tom-tom of the dwarfs, I would get up and dance. What? Stay in bed when the tom-tom called you to dance? Is that possible? And so I danced in my room, just as the hunchbacked dwarfs did over there, in the public square. Yes, those dwarfs were hunchbacked, and all it took for you to become hunchbacked too was to sing their song and dance their dance.

One glorious night, when the moon was riding high over stark-white clouds, the dwarfs returned in their customary way, and sang a song that had never been heard before. A song that carried you away, that intoxicated you. And then, of course, there was the tom-tom! That night everything seemed to have been calculated to bring the men out of their houses. The call was irresistible. They held fast to the bedsteads and door frames to keep from going outside. Their wives held them back by their feet. As for me, I was pushed out of my bed and hut, and thrown outside. In one leap, I found myself among the dwarfs, who circled about me.

"What do you want here?"

"I was take . . . take . . . taking a walk," I stammered. That seemed to cheer and appease them, and win them over.

"You were taking a walk?"

"But weren't you dancing our dance?"

"To tell you the truth, it . . . it was your singing which . . . which drew me," I said to them. "I would like to be a part of . . . a part of your group."

"But creatures like you don't sing the song or dance the dance of the dwarfs."

"I, for one, would like to learn them."

"All right. But be careful not to sing these songs and dance these dances when we're not here. If you disobey us, you'll find that"—and they showed me their humps—"you'll have one on your back too; and all your wives will run away from you, because they are 'jewels that must never be left to tarnish,' because they have an unaccountable loathing for ugliness. . . ."

"How many wives do you have to talk like that?"

"Two, three, not more."

"Well, in my case, I have entire villages. What you say is wrong; women always look for the grain of beauty in a face, the tiny flash of light, the thin thread of. . . ."

"Ananzè, let's get back to the subject of singing and dancing. . . ."

"Women, ugliness. . . ."

"We'll teach you, but. . . ."

"I understand. . . ."

And I entered into the dance. I moved my body around, lifting one leg after the other: "*Su-boum-ka!*" and nudged that one with my elbow while I thumped this one on the head: "*Su-boum! boum! Su-boum-ka!*"

At the end of several days, I had learned to sing and dance better than the admiring dwarfs.

At daybreak, they went back to their house; and inside my own, I hummed those songs that buzzed in my ears and fluttered about me. How I tried to drive them away! But they came back to perch on my lips; they kept going in and out of my mouth. I tried to clench my teeth, but they kept separating on me. . . . A woman and a melody! Who can resist them? I started singing. Having become a masterful dancer, I figured that the warning had been lifted; the taboo made null and void. I thought that the only thing I needed to do before I could break the dwarfs' law without fear of reprisal was to attain a certain position; that with my gold, I could ward off the evil. . . .

> *Su-boum! Su-boum-ka!*
> *Su-boum! boum! Su-boum-ka!*

That night we danced until dawn. . . . And, as the dwarfs departed for their village, they each whispered to me: "Ananzè, don't dance our dance anymore."

Day came, a glorious one. One of those days that, for no reason at all, brings joy to your heart, fills you with energy, and makes you want to keep moving. Everything in nature was musiclike and enchanting, a fairyland of peace and tranquility. One would have wished for it to last and last.

Yes, it was one of those days that had dawned. The birds, admiring themselves more than usual, hummed cheerfully; the leaves rustled calmly; and the roosters launched rousing cock-a-doodle-doos. Chickens clucked, and were followed by their chirping young. Ducks who looked like important personages never in a hurry tacked about like ships without a rudder. A peacock was all puffed out with his own importance and turned round himself. And there were birds in the sky, and birds in the flowering trees. . . .

I had the song in my throat, like a hiccup. I drank goblets of water to drown it. But it came back, and then left, flying off over there, on the trail polished by men and rainwaters, to join up again with the dwarfs' refrain.

I took a step . . . two steps. . . . Nothing. I turned round myself, like that. . . . Don't you do it too! . . . Still nothing.

Ah! those bluffing dwarfs! They thought they had me; yes, me,

Kacou Ananzè. The sun laughed. I sang and danced. But a strange thing happened: the more I kept dancing, and the more the sun laughed, the more I felt something on my shoulders, there, on my back. A weight. A burden. I was forced to bend over despite myself. It was impossible to stand up straight. The handsome and svelte devil that I was shrank away, and a mountain of flesh sprang up on my back.

"Hey! you on my back, come down! Do you think that I'm going to carry you while I dance the dance of the dwarfs? If you want to watch me dance, get down then and watch. . . . You turn around like that, to the right, when the tom-tom sounds: '*Su-boum-ka!*' and like that again, but to the left, arms out like this, the neck extended a bit, your body arched, and your legs bowed this way, when the tom-tom goes: '*Su-boum-boum! ka! Su-boum!*' "

Whoever was on my back did not answer. On the contrary, he weighed on me even more.

"Come on now, get down, you! Boy are you stupid! If you weren't, you'd have climbed down, and together we'd have danced the dance of the dwarfs."

But the hump climbed up on my neck, grabbed hold of my collar bones, and clamped onto my ribs. I struggled.

The hump was on my back. What could I do? I dug a hole in the kitchen floor and lay down on my back; I pretended to have a fever. I was lying there shivering when my wives returned from the fields.

"Get out of there," my youngest wife said to me.

"Leave me alone."

"How can I leave you alone when you're lying on my kitchen floor?"

"Leave me alone, I tell you!"

"Aren't you eating today?"

"I'm not hungry."

"Well the rest of us are; we're hungry. Now get up from there."

"Woman, don't touch me . . . the hump, the hunchback. . . ."

"What did you say? Hump? What hump? Who's hunchbacked?"

"You're going to make me hunchbacked. . . ."

All of those hungry women came running up, and taking me by the arms, the legs, and the head, pulled me from my hole. And the hump came forth. They hooted at me instead of pitying me. Ah! if only they had been content to hoot at me! But no. They told the neighbor woman about it, and she told her neighbor; this one told that one; that one told the other one; the other one told. . . . By the end of the day, the whole village knew that I was hunchbacked.

And since then, the sound of the dwarfs' tom-tom has echoed in my ears:

> *Su-boum! Su-boum! boum-ka!*
> *Su-boum! Su-boum-ka!*

L'ENFANT TERRIBLE

Once upon a time all the animals lived together in a village of their own, not far from the village of men. And since the men and the animals understood each other, there never was war between them.

But there was a poor man in this village of men who, in order to get to his field, had to travel a road that ran right through the village of animals. Each time he passed, they would try to pick a quarrel with him.

Sometimes it was the black monkey who came up to pull on his beard; and sometimes it was the red monkey who set traps for him. Often he found the passageway strewn with thorns. The man went on through anyway, because the war between the men and the animals had not yet been declared.

Although he was poor, this man had a wife. They both loved each other to such an extent that they would be thinking the same thing at the same moment. And this woman would always bring the noon meal to her husband in the field. The animals would watch her pass. They did not dare to try wooing her a bit, for on this subject men were known to be uncompromising. Not even the slightest teasing either. And the woman would walk on. She would say a "Good morning" here, a "Good morning" there; and the animals would say their "Good mornings" to her. And so it was: the woman would go, and the woman would come. Then she became pregnant and gave birth to a boy. He was a true phenomenon. As soon as he came out of his mother's stomach, he asked to carry the noon meal to his father. And he whistled as he went, the meal balanced on his head. When he arrived in the village of the animals, he encountered the doe. They looked at each other slowly and deliberately, the same insolence showing on both sides. The doe would have liked very much to pick a quarrel with this snip of a man. But she was alone; all the animals were in the fields. And besides, this snip of a man who was only one day old, alone, and carrying the noon meal to his father, had said nothing to her that really amounted to anything. And so, the child kept on going. But he had an idea of his own in mind.

When he arrived in the village of animals on his way back home, he met up again with the doe, who was preparing her meal.

"Little Doe, wouldn't you like to cook this yam for me?"

"Cook a yam for you? Go and give it to your mother."

"Rude little Doe, wouldn't you like to cook this yam for me?"

"You can eat it raw. I've no time to waste; if you're determined to amuse yourself, go and do it with children your own age," replied the doe who began blowing on the fire.

With one swift kick, the angry child overturned the kettle, extinguished the fire, assaulted the doe, and tied her up. He then continued on his way.

Evening came, and when the other animals returned, they found the doe bound up and moaning. The meal was nowhere to be seen. Nor was the fire.

"What happened?" asked all the animals at once.

Untied then, but still trembling and still imagining she saw that little snip of a man everywhere, the doe recounted the scene that had passed between her and the one-day-old child.

"A child one day old?" exclaimed all the animals in unison. "And he put you in the state we found you in? Where's your strength? your courage? Come now, since when has a man beat an animal in a fight? How, then, could a child one day old put you in the state we found you in? You disgrace us, Doe, really disgrace us."

The next morning, the panther stayed behind in the village. She wanted to see this phenomenal child. With long supple strides she went from one end of the village to the other, her claws finely sharpened and all exposed. The child was not late in coming.

As soon as she saw him, the panther swatted her tail against her flanks, which made such a noise that the birds, all together in one swift move, rose from the trees. This tail-lashing displaced so much air that all the fruit came down for miles and miles around. But the whistling child two days old continued on his way without getting excited, the meal balanced on his head.

The panther showed her fangs; her eyes threw out flames. The child kept whistling and laughing, and passed on by. The panther watched him disappear into the bush. . . .

She was seated and preparing her meal when this two-day-old child retraced his steps, saying: "Little Panther, wouldn't you like to cook this yam for me?"

"Me cook a yam for you? Don't you know who I am?"

"But you're just a little panther."

"You're so little yourself that you haven't yet heard about me. What do you expect? Only two days old! When you're only two days old, what do you know about the world?"

"I know more about it than you do, little Panther. Will you cook this yam for me? Yes or no?"

"I don't want to," replied the panther, who lashed her flanks with her warlike tail as she bared her sharp-pointed claws.

The kettle on the fire chattered. It whistled, raising the lid first on one side, and then on the other; it dribbled, and the froth fell into the fire, making a *chui!* . . . *chui!* sound like burning grease. That gave the panther bright ideas as she boiled with anger. This two-day-old child must have good fat on him, very tender meat; and look how plump he is, how roly-poly.

Stepping up to the fire, the child put his yam on the embers. The panther withdrew the tuber and threw it far away. The child put a second yam on the embers. Just as the panther was ready to withdraw it, he gave her a swift kick. The panther sprang up, outraged. To kick the panther—why that meant war between the men and the animals.

She approached! There she was, pouncing on the two-day-old baby. But *clouc!* the child capped her with the pot that had been boiling on the fire, then went home, whistling.

When the animals returned that evening, they found the scalded panther wounded here and wounded there . . . wounds whose scars she still retains on her fur. And she was whimpering under her cooking-pot hat. The pot was removed, and she recounted her story.

This turn of events became truly alarming. How could a two-day-old child accomplish so many feats? And where would he be in a week, in two months, or even a year, the way things were going?

The animals held a meeting. Some suggested leaving the area; others preferred resistance. And the resistance camp won. After the panther, it was the monkey's turn to stay in the village and experience this phenomenal child, then came the chameleon, the wart hog, the buffalo, the elephant, and the lion. But all of them were beaten and ill-treated by the child. The animals no longer knew what to do. They had all been defeated by this child, the big ones as well as the little ones. But how could they leave without taking up the gauntlet? without managing to beat that kid one single time? The men would be gloating over this! And they would never leave the animals alone anymore. Viewing this baby who was only several days old as the most deadly scourge of their race, the animals were determined to master it. But who now was going to stay in the village? They all looked at one another. The lion lowered his head, the panther scratched her legs, the monkey played with a piece of fruit, the elephant with a weed. Each one seemed to be following his own thoughts. The tortoise brought out her head and, facing the embarrassed areopagus, said: "I'd like to stay in the village."

All the animals burst out laughing. Can you see the tortoise succeeding where the lion, the monkey, and the elephant could not?

"You want to stay in the village?"

"Yes."

"All right, but call us if he comes back. We must finish with this child once and for all."

This decision made, the animals left for the fields.

Clouk! clak! clouk! clak! The tortoise went from one end of the village to the other. As soon as she saw the child approach, she ran toward him; and holding herself erect on her little feet, with her neck outstretched, a humble look in her eye, and a respectful attitude, she entered into a conversation.

"Good morning, my master, you who are the strongest of men."

"Good morning, you intelligent tortoise."

"Here, give me your load! It'll be an honor for me to carry it for you. I'll accompany you for a bit of the way. What news do you bring from the village of men? The harvest isn't good here. The rain doesn't fall. Next year, perhaps, things will be otherwise; and we'll invite all you men to the great festival we have after the harvest. Oh! how we dance! I'm the one who plays the great big tom-tom. . . . On that day. . . . Well, here we are, at the edge of the village. . . . I'd like very much to go a bit farther . . . but there are limits to how far I can go, boundaries."

After giving the platter back to the phenomenal child, the tortoise
went to hide near a cottage. As soon as he reappeared, she quickly, very
quickly, accosted him: "That yam, give it here. . . . The ashes are hot.
I was waiting for you over there so that I could take your beautiful yam
and prepare it for you."

She took the tuber and cooked it. It was peeled carefully and cut in
half, then placed in a clean bowl containing onions, crushed red pep-
pers, some salt and palm-oil, and a bit of dried fish that had been grilled
on the fire.

The child ate and drank. After thanking the intelligent tortoise, he
went on his way.

Once the child had gone, the tortoise armed herself with a hoe and
began plowing up the ground in the village.

When the animals returned that evening, they saw holes everywhere.

"What happened, Tortoise?"

"You can see what happened. You had scarcely turned your backs
when this phenomenon of a youngster came up to me more arrogant
than ever. He grabbed me by the neck, and I took him by the waist. We
struggled, and kept on struggling. He threw me down over here, and
I threw him over there; he knocked me over, and I knocked him over in
turn. The sun was right there, level with our heads. But we still kept
on fighting."

"You were able to hold your own with this child?"

"The sun had disappeared; it was hidden behind the trees, and we
were still battling. Look at all those holes; they're our marks. . . . Ah!
my friends! This snip of a man is truly a phenomenon. And he promised
to come back."

"To come back?"

"Alas, my friends, it's true. He wants to gain the victory that I
refused him. . . ."

As they listened to the tortoise tell of her adventures, the lion, the panther, the elephant, and the buffalo—all those powerful beasts of the jungle—anxiously thought of their own crown. . . . "If all the tortoises form a coalition against us, we won't be the mighty rulers anymore. . . ." And they began to yawn, as if to tell the tortoise that she could bring an end to her tale. But the tortoise continued on: "I wanted to avenge our king the lion, our master the panther."

"Enough!" thundered the lion, smarting under the reminder.

"Yes, he did promise to come back."

The tortoise was still talking when the child reappeared. The animals perked up. The monkey, swinging from branch to branch, drifted away; the lion crept about; the buffalo slipped into the bushes; the elephant edged himself in between some trees, his trunk lowered under his belly; and the panther glided between the liana vines without even grazing them. They went their way without even looking behind them, without worrying at all about the fate of their numerous subjects. They ran and ran, and when they dared to stop running, each one found himself alone.

From that day on, the animals have no longer lived together in a village of their own; hatred, too, has sprung up between them and man.

After that, when, at the slightest noise, the Capuchin monkey sends out his alarm: "*Kpa-koum!*" the bush immediately falls silent again.

It watches, and scrutinizes, and questions.

SPIDER'S OX

God had a field that was full of brambles and brushwood. Brambles and brushwood were so entangled that even the serpents themselves had fled the place.

The crickets were silent in this suffocating darkness. And the butterflies would try to pass over this field without having to alight. Pitched against the sky, the thorns resembled huge, tapering sword points. And rain or shine, brambles and brushwood grew without stopping.

This was God's field.

A rather unusual and massive silk-cotton tree grew in this field; a big, thorny silk-cotton tree that must have been the ancestor of all silk-cotton trees, for it was so very crooked and ungainly, so twisted and corkscrewlike. Frightful it was, something hideous in the way of trees. The birds never landed on this field. Even the sun glided on by, while the breeze skirted it altogether. One wonders how God, who always has such an accurate eye, could let loose from his hands such a monster. People would look at the moon, the stars, and the ocean; they would listen to the humming of the wind and the chattering of the breeze; they would admire the graceful flight of the birds and the butterflies; and then, turning their heads toward the silk-cotton tree, would say to themselves: "Come on now, really! even God could have done better than this! All those marvels to look at, and over there, that monster of a silk-cotton tree!"

The men would whisper that morning and evening, day and night. All the time. Even the birds would say it to each other in their various warblings.

Butterflies would repeat it in their flight; and whenever they alighted, their wings fluttering, they would still be talking about the silk-cotton tree.

The setting sun and the rising moon, the breeze when it awakened from its nap, the ebb and flow of the tide—they all were interested in that twisted and misshapen, ungainly, leprous silk-cotton tree.

Everything in nature talked so much about this tree that God decided to have it cut down. Cut down? Yes . . . but not with an axe, nor with cutting irons! Well then, with what? . . . With . . . how should I say this . . . with . . . with that.

Can one cut down a tree with . . . that?

Evidently no one wanted to put it to a test, for the silk-cotton tree continued to grow in its field of brambles and brushwood. God's decision was repeated more than a thousand times. But no one came forward. Cut down a tree with that? Do you really think it could be done? Heralds had run about the world more than a thousand times. And no one had come forward to say: "I'll do it; I'll cut down the silk-cotton tree with that . . . and nothing but that." And the twisted silk-cotton tree, knowing that no one would ever step forward, insolently shook its stumplike branches. It shook them as if to taunt the men. It tore at the howling wind and slashed at the sun which went to bed all bleeding.

The heralds had cried out the news more than ten thousand times, and when all the males looked over there, they would murmur: "Cut down the tree, we agree, but really now! not with that!" And so the tree remained there, sunshine and rain, shaking its stumplike branches in the wind.

The appointed time was about to pass when, one morning, Kacou Ananzè presented himself before God.

"What news have you brought me, Ananzè?"

"The people on earth are in good health."

"And yet, complaints often reach me."

"It's nothing. . . . It's a sign that they are happy, that they are thinking of you."

"What fairy tale is this you're telling me, Kacou Ananzè?"

"You don't know the people because you live so far away from them. . . . As for me, I know them as well as I know myself."

"And you, what will become of you?"

"What will become of me? If only I knew that myself! Life has become monotonous; there is no longer any occasion to show yourself, to prove your intelligence. When I came home after a very long voyage, I found out that you wanted to knock down your silk-cotton tree."

"Yes, but with that. . . ."

"Why that's not even a challenge! And you've found no one to offer to do it?"

"Not a single man."

"Well, I myself am going to knock down that silk-cotton tree, and with nothing but that. Anyhow, we've got to show everyone that you did create intelligent beings, that you filled your world with clever people. Knock down a tree with that? . . . But that's easy."

"You could do that, could you?"

"If not, I wouldn't have come."

"If you'd do it, I could boast about having created people. I put all the ugliness of the world into that silk-cotton tree, so that my creatures would be beautiful and perfect. Now, no one talks about anything but that twisted and misshapen, one-armed silk-cotton tree that looks like a corkscrew. The sun talks about it; the moon talks about it; man talks about it; even the breeze and the wind, the stars, the ebb and flow of the tide, and the swallow do—everyone has talked so much about it that I finally said to myself: 'It must be knocked down.' "

"And you want it done with that?"

"Yes. . . ."

"It'll be a mere game."

"Look. Do you see that ox over there? It's the most beautiful beast in my herds. It'll be your reward."

"You might as well have it taken to my house, for your silk-cotton tree is already knocked down."

"Already knocked down?"

"I mean, I've already won the bet. When do you want me to begin?"

"When you will, this evening, tomorrow, the day after. . . . Wait, I almost forgot. Let me know when you want to start so that I can have you accompanied."

"You mean, watched?"

"By one of my children."

"It'll be tomorrow . . . in the morning."

When night came, Kacou Ananzè went to the foot of the tree to hide a hatchet that he had been sharpening for two months.

As soon as daylight crept into his hut, he got up, and without even washing himself, ran toward the silk-cotton tree where the child already waited. He erected the scaffolding, climbed up onto it, took off his clothes, and began to work, singing: "*Han! Han! Han!* God's ox, I'm going to have it.

"*Han!* where should I eat it?

"*Han!* How thirsty I am! How thirsty! How thirsty!

"*Han!* Little one, give me something to drink."

"I don't have any water, Papa Ananzè."

"*Han!* How thirsty I am! How thirsty! How thirsty!

"I'm going to die of thirst. I'm dying of thirst, thirst, thirst. Little one, would you go and find me some water?"

"Gladly."

And Kacou Ananzè handed him a basket. And the child left to look for water.

As soon as he had his back turned, our butcher took the hatchet, and *pan! pan! pan!* The massive silk-cotton tree was disappearing in huge splinters. Sap was flowing from everywhere, and it was as red as human blood this sap from the thorny and twisted silk-cotton tree. And the blood flowed out from all the veinletlike holes which throng the wood of the silk-cotton tree. And the sun had become red, so red, so very red. With each blow of the hatchet, the tree rustled its stumplike branches despairingly, as if to ask for mercy. But Kacou Ananzè kept striking with force; he kept striking with fury. He had the ox to win. He wanted to beat God with his tricks. The tree began to cry, to howl, to bend under the pain. Its fibers split. Kacou Ananzè kept pounding.

But the child was coming back, with the basket on his head.

"What's going on there? Where's the water?"

"The container is no good. Water keeps flowing out from everywhere."

"You're nothing but a little scamp. I'm going to tell God about this. Look how I'm perspiring, and you can't even bring me a bit of water to drink. Do you want me to die?"

And *han! han!* he began again to strike the silk-cotton tree with only that.

The child stood there, crying. . . .

"So, you're crying now, are you? Haven't you cried long enough? It's I who should cry. Do you think it's easy to knock down a tree with only this?"

"No, I was only looking at you. . . ."

"Ah! you were just looking at me. . . . So haven't you ever seen me before? Are you going to just stand there and look at me like that? Get along! run quickly and find me some water."

And the child went off again toward the stream, armed with another basket.

Taking up the hatchet again, he continued his work. The silk-cotton tree begged for mercy. But Kacou Ananzè kept hitting away. The silk-cotton tree was bending; it was bowing. Ananzè kept hitting. The stumplike branches trembled in pain; the blood flowed in fits and starts. With all of his passions unleashed, Ananzè struck harder than ever.

Finally . . . *Kpakpa . . . chuii . . . touhoum* . . . the misshapen silk-cotton tree, the twisted and leprous, corkscrewlike silk-cotton tree that housed all the ugliness of the world, fell. The wind then began blowing violently.

It is said that with this fall, all the ugliness in the world was set free, that it spread throughout the universe in this howling wind.

The child returned the moment the tree went crashing down, and he testified before God that Kacou Ananzè had not in any way used a hatchet, or a cutting iron of any sort, that he had used only "that."

The ox was handed over to our hero who went away, singing:

> "God, yes God, you really can trick him.
> All you need is plenty of guts.
> God, yes God, you really can trick him.
> He is so old that he doesn't see a thing.
> I knocked down the silk-cotton tree with that.
> When has a tree ever been knocked down with only that?
> We too are intelligent, yes we are.
> God, yes God, he too can be tricked.
> We too are intelligent, oh yes we are."

And he went on his way. He passed through villages and more villages, forests and more forests, crossed over oceans and more oceans, plains, and deserts. He kept moving because he wanted to be alone when he ate the ox; he wanted to be all by himself. An ant would not touch a morsel of it; a fly would not even perch on a bit of it to rub its legs. If only he could prevent the wind from carrying off the scent! But if he went and asked that idiot of a wind to stop all its blowing, it would immediately start chattering in the leaves, raising dust, and churning up everything on the ground. The wind? He would catch it. He would trap it and throw it far away. . . .

Kacou Ananzè continued his travels, slackening his pace from time to time to outwit the flies that kept appearing. As soon as he slowed down, they would come charging, "*Vouhoum!*" And Kacou Ananzè would immediately set off again. Finally, he came to a place where not even a single ant had left a trace. He continued on, however, for he was determined to be alone when he ate his ox.

When, that evening, he slowed down as he approached a clearing, some ichneumons came rushing up. If the wind is refused the scent of a meal, you can eat without being bothered by those ichneumons, those abortions of a fly. Ananzè walked on.

Finally, he came to a quiet spot, a spot so quiet and peaceful in fact that he was afraid for the first time in his life. Nothing here stirred. Everything seemed to be made of stone. No gnats, not even the slightest insect.

"I'll eat my ox right here," Kacou Ananzè said to himself.

To kill it, to cut it up, to put it in a pot and prepare it was a matter of an hour or more. . . . He was getting ready to eat when, all of a sudden, something fell from the sky.

"That must be the drink. An ox as fat as this one is always eaten with a good palm-wine. For sure it must be an earthenware pot filled with wine that God sends me. Really now, he thinks of everything!"

Kacou Ananzè rushed toward the spot where the object had fallen. . . .

"And who are you?"

"I'm your host."

"What host? Did you help me knock down the silk-cotton tree with that, just to be my host?"

"God sends me to keep you company because you're in my kingdom."

"You'll allow me to leave here then?"

"Never. . . ."

"Let's understand each other right off. I'm in your territory; therefore, I'm your guest. You owe me hospitality."

"Agreed, but that won't prevent us from sharing what you have over there . . . that meal of yours which mustn't be touched by a single fly, and whose scent, moreover, mustn't be carried off by the wind."

"Follow me."

"I don't walk anywhere. One carries me."

"And who's going to carry you?"

"You are."

"Me? Kacou Ananzè? carry a nasty monster like you? Why you're as flabby and as sticky as snot."

"You'll carry me."

"But I won't."

"In this case, if you don't carry me, you won't be able to escape. Your feet will break, your head will split, and you'll be hunchbacked."

Despite the threats, Kacou Ananzè wanted to walk away anyhow, but he felt his feet cracking, his head splitting, and a hump pushing itself up on his back. He was forced, therefore, to shoulder that foul being who was nothing other than Death.

As soon as he arrived near the meal, he threw him down, *floc!* and wanted to start eating. But the monster said to him: "If you touch that dish, you'll die."

And Kacou Ananzè watched him eat by himself the ox that he himself had cleverly won. And he thought to himself: "No, I guess God can't be fooled as easily as that after all."

Happily sated, Death fell asleep and began snoring. Kacou Ananzè set fire to the straw mat, and Death, who was nothing but fat, melted.

"So there! You ate my ox. Now I'm going to eat you. That's justice."

And putting a finger in the fat, he then brought it to his mouth. The fat fell onto his tongue which grew bigger and bigger and blacker and blacker all the time.

But Kacou Ananzè hardly lost his head over such a small thing. A bigger tongue? Is that a calamity?

A few days later, Ananzè called together all the animals for a feast, at the beginning of which he arranged a swimming contest. All the animals came. But in order to swim, he had to deposit his tongue on the bank. The animals trusted him and deposited their tongues on the bank too.

The dog even deposited his tongue. But at the precise moment they were to throw themselves into the water, the ever-watchful dog took out one of his eyes and placed it next to his tongue.

While the animals were happily swimming, Ananzè climbed out of the water and went to grab hold of the dog's tongue. But the eye was there, watching him, following his every move. . . .

"You there, Dog, you'll never be able to enjoy yourself. You have eyes all over the place. Did you think that I was coming to take your tongue? I was only looking at it."

Ananzè took the sheep's tongue, put his in its place, and went back to join the others. Scarcely had he put his feet in the water when he gave the signal to start. Every animal found his tongue except the sheep.

"My tongue, who took my tongue?"

"But there it is," replied Kacou Ananzè.

"That's not mine."

"Tongue for tongue, take it . . . for each of us has his own."

The sheep was obliged to take the ugly black tongue which he has worn to this very day.

SPIDER AND THE TORTOISE

It happened during a famine. An atrocious famine, unique of its kind. And it lasted for years. A severe and persistent famine that had settled on the hillsides and the mountains, in the valleys, the bush, and in the villages. It was felt everywhere, and everywhere it was up to its old tricks. It even prevented the rain from falling. And since the rain did not fall, the waters, in an effort to resist, withdrew onto their beds; the trees, trying to hold out, shed their leaves and cast off their branches. No longer did a single young shoot spring up at the feet of any of those forest giants who loved to capture the sun and the rain and distribute them in rays, or in drops, all around.

In order to remain alive, Kacou Ananzè had learned to set traps. But, as if famished and without strength themselves, his traps could catch nothing. Nonetheless, every morning he went to visit them. The traps remained bent timber. Not even one that happened to be erect in its slip-knot offered him any prey whatsoever. He wouldn't have cared what he caught. . . . But no, the stubborn traps remained bent.

Ananzè no longer knew just what trick to invent to catch something in one of his many traps. He would be happy with a butterfly, a cricket, or an earthworm—even with a foul-smelling dung beetle. . . . But the stubborn traps remained bent.

One morning, reeling with hunger, he went to visit those contrivances of his. From a distance he could see that one of the traps was erect; a black speck moved at the end of the line, and kept moving. His heart took off at a gallop, anxious to see what that speck could be. Finally, said Kacou Ananzè to himself, today there'll be something to sink my teeth into.

With machete in hand, he advanced; as he approached, he saw a squirrel hanging there at the end of the line, a beautiful squirrel, plump and glistening of fat, with a fine bushy tail, and long, stiff, tidy whiskers. A squirrel who must have come from far away.

"A squirrel for my dinner, God be thanked! It's a tender meat. A good sauce and there's nothing like it!" And he clicked his tongue.

With the machete raised, he grabbed the squirrel by the head and stood ready to cut off its neck.

"Ananzè, don't kill me. I can do you good."

"Good? What good can you do for me? The only good you can do for me is to fill up my stomach, to let me eat you. . . ."

"Your stomach will be filled. Save me, and you'll see. I'm from a very rich country where we don't know what famine is."

"Where do you come from?"

"From a country not far from here, and I was on my way to see my wife's family in the village down the road from yours."

"What village down the road? On this side there is no village."

"Ananzè, don't kill me, and you'll be happy."

"Just wait! I'm going to save you in such a way that your head will soon be in my cooking pot."

And Ananzè began to sharpen his machete, which made a sound like "*Cochio! cochio! cochio! cochio!*" And the squirrel swayed back and forth at the far end of the trap, compelled to listen to the sad music of a machete that very soon would make the blood come forth and stream down his throat. He saw his blood being sucked in by the parched earth, and he shuddered. But Kacou Ananzè, touching his index finger to the edge of the machete, resumed his work: "*Cochio! cochio!*"

"Ananzè, you're my brother."

"You? my brother? Since when is Ananzè the Spider the brother of the squirrel?"

"I'm from your mother's village."

"My mother! My mother! She's dead. Therefore, she has no more village."

"*Cochio! cochio!*" went the machete, sharper now than a sword's blade.

"I knew your mother. She often spoke to me of you."

"You certainly may be from my mother's village, but not from my village. And even if you were from my own village, do you think that your head still wouldn't be at the bottom of my cooking pot?"

"How good your mother was!"

"As good and sweet as the hearth's flame that will soon caress your skin."

"Ananzè, I assure you, undo the line around my feet and grab me by the tail. I'll lead you to the most beautiful, the most marvelous of countries. Try to picture it. Only try. Grab my tail. Harder. Can I escape?"

"No."

"Undo the line."

Kacou Ananzè removed the line from the squirrel's feet. And they immediately set off, crossing over hillsides and mountains, valleys, rivers, and oceans, even the densest of forests. He had become dizzy, poor Ananzè, but the squirrel kept going.

They passed by a field of ripe papayas.

"Squirrel, do you see those beautiful papayas?"

"Those? Why they're nothing."

"Nothing? those beautiful papayas whose perfume I smell? I want to eat some."

"Don't let go of my tail."

"My God! what a country! You see those papayas, don't you? Don't you understand when I say I'm hungry? No! when one has such beautiful whiskers and a skin glistening with fat, one doesn't understand such language."

"Don't let go of my tail. We haven't arrived yet. Ahead of us are even lusher regions."

The smell of the papayas was sweet and mild; it was *moukoun-moukoun*[1] and delicate.

With their color, their smell, and their quivering leaves, the papayas seemed to be saying: "Stop, Kacou Ananzè! Let go of the squirrel's tail!"

"Don't let go of my tail. As I said, there are even lusher regions ahead of us."

"Where ahead of us? I adore papayas, and I want to eat some."

"Just a short step left to go and we'll be at my house. Those papayas you say? Why they grow on vacant land where my children defecate."

A field of maize extended for miles and miles, as far as the eye could see. Maize with white beards and russet beards; fresh maize that was so good to eat.

"That's my young wife's field."

A huge field of yams came next, as big as all outdoors.

"That field belongs to my young wife's daughter."

A field of ripe bananas then appeared. Kacou Ananzè could hold himself back no longer. At the sight of all this food, the insides of his

---

1 "Subtle" in the N'Zima dialect: meant to summarize all the adjectives in the sentence.—Dadié's note

stomach writhed. Oh for some of those ripe bananas that the monkeys and bats were eating! And he was eating all this only with his eyes.

"That field belongs to my youngest child."

"Who are you, Squirrel, to have so much wealth?"

"Don't let go of my tail."

"My mother spoke often of you and your riches. But I didn't know you. Oh how God makes things turn out right! If this famine hadn't occurred when it did, would I have ever known you? And known that you came from my mother's village? Alas! my good mother who died too soon! She spoke of you even when she was dying."

"Don't let go of my tail. We'll soon be home."

"Hunger and misery can make one do some pretty stupid things, you know. At times, my stomach spoke louder than my mind. If I weren't good-natured, if the blood that binds us hadn't spoken so strongly, I would have killed a brother at this very hour. Squirrel, forget what I said. . . ."

A sugar-cane forest. Spider could really hold out no longer. Huge sugar-cane stalks in blossom, and singing! The leaves were caressing each other, holding each other up. And what wonderful whisperings when the wind blew!

"Don't let go of my tail."

How beautiful they are, those sugar-cane stalks! And juicy too! That you can feel from a distance; you need only look at their joints— they are as big as arms. And they are emitting such a sweet aroma. . . .

Finally! It was time. The right time. A little bit farther, and Spider let go of the tail.

There they were in the village of the squirrel, who recounted his entire adventure to his family, stressing in particular the innate goodness and generosity of Kacou Ananzè.

To receive him, they killed more than a thousand beef. As for the goats, chickens, guinea-cocks, sheep, and ducks—one no longer counted them. There was no time for it. Dishes were everywhere, some here, some there, so many in fact that one no longer knew where to put them. And yet they kept coming. Ananzè ate, and ate still more. He would have wished to have a more voluminous stomach, and to fill it with all those succulent dishes that kept coming all the time. But he had only a spider's stomach.

Young girls came to sing for him, young boys to dance. He forgot his own village, the famine, and the traps. For the very first time, he congratulated himself on having been so kind. He whispered to himself: "Oh how nice it is to do good! If I had killed the squirrel, would I have had all this?" And he ate and ate. His stomach was stretched to bursting. He ate anyhow. Whenever he thought of the severe and persistent famine that had settled on the hillsides and the mountains, in the valleys, the bush, and the villages, he would stuff himself until it hurt. He ate, happy to eat, happy to take his revenge on the famine.

As it happened, however, bad luck was soon to begin for him, for behind the squirrel's concession was the tortoise's house. A ram comprised her entire fortune, the type with many horns, and the only food she ate was a maize gruel. To amuse herself all day long, the tortoise would provoke the village children to fight. She kept shouting: "It's me, the tortoise! The most courageous tortoise in the world. Who wants to fight me? Who wants to pit himself against me? No one will ever beat me in battle, ever. Why I'll even offer my ram to the one who beats me."

And Kacou Ananzè watched the tortoise strutting about; he heard her boasting. The ram was truly handsome, one of those with many horns, and with a coat of hair that dragged the ground. And he wanted to have that ram. The first two days he laughed at the bragging, but on the third day, when the idea to possess that ram took root in his head, laughter gave way to anger.

"What is she saying, that tortoise there?" he asked between bitefuls.

"She's not talking about you," replied the squirrel.

"All the same, tell her to stop; I'm not much on challenges. So she's never been beaten in battle, has she? Who, tell me, has never been beaten? Well, in my country neither have I; no one has ever beaten me in battle. And I defy anyone who thinks he can."

"Calm yourself and eat. It's her song. She hasn't sung anything but that since she was born."

"Her song, or not her song, to me that song is a challenge. Tell her to stop."

"You're right. But calm yourself and eat. The tortoise is a mad-woman. Everyone in the village knows that."

"Well, if she continues, I'm going to cure her of this madness."

At the entrance to her hut, the tortoise shouted at the top of her voice so as to be heard over the drum noise and the singing of the young girls: "It's me, the tortoise, the most courageous tortoise in the world. Who wants to fight me? I'll offer my ram to the winner."

"I'll have that ram," Kacou Ananzè said to himself. "I'll take that tortoise by the shell, like that, and turn her over, like this, with her legs in the air, and there, she'll be beaten. And I'll come away with the ram and a reputation to boot."

He raised a scuffle with anyone who tried to hold him back. There he was, planted in front of the tortoise.

"Who are you talking about?"

"Not about you, stranger. You don't know me, and I don't know you. How could I talk about you? I play with the village children. . . ."

"Hasn't one of them ever beaten you?"

"Never! And not a single person in this village will ever beat me."

"That's a challenge. To utter such nonsense in front of a wrestling champion like me—go ahead and admit that this is a challenge."

"But no! This doesn't concern you, stranger."

"Back home where I live, we don't talk that way. And I don't like for anyone near me to talk like that. I'd love to do battle with you. . . . So no one has ever beaten you in battle you say. Well, today you're going to be beaten."

"Who is the person who'll beat me?"

"Me, Kacou Ananzè."

"You? But I wasn't talking about you at all."

"But I say that you were talking about me. Since I'm here in this village, what you say concerns me too. If you hadn't wanted to include me, you should've said: 'No one in this village can beat me, except Papa Kacou Ananzè.' "

"But since I didn't mention you, and since we've never fought. . . ."

"That's what I said! You must have wanted us to fight. You confess to the challenge then."

"I swear I don't. However, if you're determined to fight me, try it, and you'll see."

"Try it and I'll see? Is it you, the little tortoise, who says that to me, Kacou Ananzè the invincible? Well, you'll be the one who sees!"

And there they were, at grips. Kacou Ananzè grabbed the tortoise around the waist . . . with difficulty, yes, but he grabbed her anyway, and "crou-crou, crou-crou," they leaned this way; "crou-crou, crou-crou," they leaned that way. They leaned back over this way, then took off again over there, and finally, "téguèn zen," there was the tortoise on the ground . . . on her small feet.

"There, you're beaten, you insolent one. . . ."

"Not at all. In order to beat the tortoise, her feet have to be in the air," the onlookers shouted at him.

"Oh! never mind that."

And they took up the battle again, shaking up the sand over here, raising the dust over there.

Ananzè felt himself growing tired; he was losing his strength, and the shame was rising. How he wished that all those people watching the battle would order it stopped! But all of them, understandably taking the tortoise's side, waited for the end of the tournament. And the tortoise kept on softly singing: "It's me, the tortoise, the most courageous tortoise in the world. Who can do battle with me? No one? Not even a stranger? I'll give my ram to the winner."

The allusion was so direct that Kacou Ananzè, furious with the injury to his vanity, redoubled his efforts. They each wanted to win. An arm stretched out; a leg drew back; a neck poked forth; an opponent was squeezed as tight as possible to the other's chest so as to suffocate him before he was thrown to the ground.

The tortoise stood erect on her little tail, and with a flashing-quick gesture threw Kacou Ananzè into the air.

And where did he find himself? In his own village. He screamed: "I don't want the tortoise's ram anymore! I don't want that ram anymore!" Everyone thought him crazy. They said so even around him, as they had said about the tortoise over there, in the squirrel's village.

He told everyone about the wonders of his voyage to the land of the squirrel and about the tortoise's ram. As they heard what he said, every listener shook his head and went off convinced that he was dealing with a madman. The more he told of his adventure, the more he passed for a madman.

One morning Kacou Ananzè left the village of those other madmen who did not want to believe that beyond their own village was the squirrel's village, a place where one lived happily, where he himself, Kacou Ananzè, would have continued to live happily, surrounded by joy, abundance, and peace, if only he had not become involved with the tortoise and her ram!

And ever since then, like you who search for fortune, happiness, and peace, Kacou Ananzè searches for the road leading to the squirrel's village. He continues to set traps. But the time of the severe and persistent famine has passed. And only foolish gnats let themselves be caught. But what gnat even suspects the existence of the squirrel's village, that place where one lives in blissful abundance and joy?

And ever since that morning, Kacou Ananzè roams the bush night and day, going from leaf to leaf, branch to branch.

Lying in ambush along the sides of the footpaths, he keeps on the watch for the squirrel's passage.

On the banks of babbling springs, he dreams about the land of plenty.

Perched on the highest of peaks, he looks for the land of the squirrel where plenty and peace are kings.

MOTHER IGUANA'S FUNERAL

Iguana-Son and Kacou Ananzè Spider were friends, and their friendship had blossomed with time. Everyone was surprised by this deep and abiding friendship that seemed to overcome all obstacles. More than one pair of friends would have liked to have the same relationship, but their many thorns—always trimmed well but prickly nonetheless—prevented them from being like Iguana-Son and Kacou Ananzè. However, there were many who were forever saying to Iguana-Son: "Beware of your friend."

"Why?"

"Because he's Spider."

"Nothing more than that?"

"Beware."

"He's never done anything to me."

"Friendship with Kacou Ananzè costs dearly. With him, one always ends up a fool. He has tricked man, monkey, lion, and panther, even the elephant, the fox, and the dog. Do you think he'll spare you? Be careful! Friendship with a spider weighs as much as the friendship with someone bigger, and the ego of an upstart always comes down strong. Kacou Ananzè is nothing but an upstart; and well you know that, Iguana-Son."

"But I don't know that."

"You will, one day."

Time passed, strengthening the ties of this friendship. Evil tongues no longer talked about them. And, as if cleared of useless suckers and vine branches, their friendship blossomed prettier than ever!

But one evening, after dinner, as the people were chatting around the fire, the women on one side, the children on the other, a stranger arrived and gave them the news: Mother Iguana had just died.

Mother Iguana was the best of mothers. And her son cried and cried. He threw himself down over there and over here; he rolled around in the dust, thrashed the earth with his claws, and again with his nails, and beat his head against a wall. And he became dirty, so very dirty, that poor little Iguana who had just lost his mother. Kacou Ananzè tried to cry, but have you ever seen a spider's tears? Kacou Ananzè doesn't have any. . . .

The time had come to go to the funeral.

The preparations had been made, and because the village was far away, our two friends were off one morning at the first crowing of the cock.

Little accustomed to long outings, Iguana-Son stopped often to rest. And to keep up their courage, the two travelers sometimes sang, sometimes practiced crying, for custom has it that in such situations you cry until you reach the village.

Iguana-Son cried with such a raucous-sounding voice that Kacou Ananzè became annoyed. And he said so to Iguana-Son. Iguana-Son was hurt. He said nothing, however, and kept the wound at the bottom of his heart. Then it was Kacou Ananzè's turn to cry.

> *"Gben'zé ni a houô kagboum!*
> *Gben'zé ni a houô kagboum!"*[1]

1 Mother Iguana is dead: *kagboum!*—Dadié's note

His friend Iguana-Son looked at him and began to cry, while chanting:

*"E-ni mô su-han bè n'zu n'zô
E-lan mô bè su-han bè n'zu n'zô
Bè sun akolon minsan miahlô! . . . ô-ô
Amo zihaba miahlô . . . ô-ô!"*²

Up until then, it had never entered Kacou Ananzè's mind to play a trick on his friend. But as soon as Iguana-Son had stopped crying, had finished talking about his drunken relatives, *"akolon minsan miahlô! ô-ô!"* Kacou Ananzè said to himself: "I'll get you."

When the village came into view, Kacou said to his companion: "Let's each of us assume a new name."

"For what purpose? Your name is Kacou Ananzè, and mine's Iguana. Everyone knows us by these names, so what good is it to change them?"

"We must. For safety's sake. You know those devils and sorcerers; when they know your name, they can harm you, but with another name. . . ."

"Do you think that no one will recognize us?"

"Let's each assume a new name. Understand?"

"No, I don't understand."

"You're stupid. They've always told me so, and I'm just beginning to realize it."

That was the second wound that Kacou Ananzè had given Iguana, and Iguana kept that one too at the bottom of his heart.

---

2 When your mothers cry, they never cry like that;
When your grandmothers cry, they never cry like that.
They cry, instead: "How sad it is to be with a drunkard,
For he is the last to know grief."—Translation provided by Dadié

"Come on, let each of us assume a new name. You're going to be 'Papa Stay-Put,' and me, 'Papa Stranger.' Understood?"

"Understood."

"Agreed?"

"Agreed."

"Be sure to remember now that you're 'Papa Stay-Put' and me, 'Papa Stranger.' "

The simple of heart are so made that they hitch their feelings to any thorn in order to prove their strength. Iguana-Son had just fallen into a trap. Spider was going to teach him to insult his relatives under the pretense of tears.

As night was falling, they entered the village. It was announced that Iguana-Son had just arrived for his mother's funeral. After the tears were wept, the news told and retold, food was brought inside the hut that had been placed at the two travelers' disposal.

The young girl who brought the dishes placed them on the wooden stool that served as a table, and said:

"Here's dinner for Papa Stranger."

"What?" said Kacou Ananzè, cupping his hand hornlike over his ear to hear better, and turning toward the child, who showed no concern whatsoever.

"I bring Papa Stranger's dinner."

"Did you hear that, Iguana? It's for Papa Stranger. Isn't that what you said, little girl?"

"Yes."

Kacou Ananzè ate the food all by himself, right in the face of his friend. Iguana swallowed his saliva, as he watched his friend take mouthfuls as big as fists. That lasted for two weeks. All the dishes that were brought—and everyone in the village wanted to outdo his neighbor in generosity—therefore went to Papa Stranger, that is to say, to

Kacou Ananzè Spider. He ate them all, without giving so much as a bite to Iguana-Son. He kept eating and clicking his tongue. He would suck on a bone for hours, and lick his fingers, "*piô! piô!*" and belch loudly, "*gâhôwe!*"

"How sweet it is! I'm convinced, Iguana, that there are real cooks in this country, *piô! piô!* I think I'll come back here and take a wife, *gâhôwe!* What do you think?"

". . ."

"As you can see, my friend, the people of your village are mean. They constantly forget you when they distribute the dishes. Obviously, it's because you're Papa Stay-Put, while I'm Papa Stranger. And everyone wants to honor the stranger. Patience, my friend, perhaps it'll be your turn tomorrow."

But tomorrow came, and, as on the previous days, all of the dishes were for Papa Stranger.

Iguana-Son had become unrecognizable. So very weak! And yet he tried to dance all the time. He kept trying to dance away the hunger from his stomach. Unable to hold out any longer, he got up during the night and went to the dumps to look for something to eat. But he wasted away anyhow; his pretty, yellow-gold color began to fade. . . .

"Are you sick, Iguana?" the people asked him.

"No!"

"What's wrong with you then?"

"Nothing."

"You worry us. You'd better return to your village right away. . . . Look at your friend, how fat he gets! You've become a mere thorn. When you get back home, the people there are going to say that you had nothing to eat here."

". . ."

"Yes! Yes! Why of course! How stupid we are sometimes! It's

because you feel sad. Bah! that's life! you know! Here today, gone
tomorrow! There's really nothing so bad about it to let yourself waste
away like that."

"Hum!"

"What's wrong with you, Iguana-Son?"

"I'm worried!"

"Worried? We all have worries. Drown them in palm-wine, or in
food. When you're really stuffed, the worries haven't any door left to
enter by. We're going to increase your rations."

Iguana-Son looked at Kacou Ananzè, who interrupted, saying: "My
friend doesn't like to travel. He gets thin whenever we change locations;
and that, you can be sure, pains me a great deal. Just think! We eat
together. But it's true what people say. He gets thin, and I get fat. Evil
tongues are having a good time with this. From now on, I think it best
not to travel with my friend Iguana-Son."

"Come on now! You're not going to get worked up over a little thing
like this, are you? He's sad. That's all. The dishes are going to be so
plentiful and so varied that your friend is bound to get fat."

And, indeed, the dishes were plentiful and varied, but Iguana-Son
continued to waste away anyhow because all the young girls who
brought the meals never stopped saying: "It's for Papa Stranger."

The people no longer understood what was happening with Iguana-
Son. In similar cases, sorcerers have come and eaten people during the
night. That, however, was not the case with Iguana. For they had questioned Fate, and Fate had said that no devil would eat Iguana during the
night. Was his mother angry? "No," she had said to the sorcerers who
had intervened in the matter. Everyone in the village thus began to
search out the reason why Iguana-Son was growing thinner.

One day an old woman asked her little girl: "When you go over
there with the dishes, what do you say?"

"I say: 'Here are the dishes for Papa Stranger.' "

"And then?"

"That's all."

"What happens when you say that?"

"One of them, the fatter of the two, makes me repeat the phrase each time, as if he's deaf."

"And after that?"

"After that, he says to his friend: 'Did you hear? The dish is for Papa Stranger only.' "

"And what does the other one do?"

"The other one? He moves aside."

"Hum! I see. Tomorrow, when you take the dishes, ask the other one, the one who moves aside, what his name is."

That evening, the young girl arrived with the dishes, and placing them in front of Kacou Ananzè Spider, said: "Here's Papa Stranger's meal," and then immediately asked Iguana: "What's your name?"

"Me? I'm Papa Stay-Put."

The young girl reported that to the old woman. And that same night, Iguana-Son's name was known to all the women of the village. The next day all of the dishes arrived in the name of Papa Stay-Put.

"What? Papa Stranger or Papa Stay-Put?" exclaimed Kacou Ananzè.

"Papa Stay-Put," replied the young girls.

"Are you sure you haven't got the names wrong? Didn't your mothers tell you to say: 'Papa Stranger?' "

"They told us: 'Papa Stay-Put.' "

"You're confusing the two names. Surely they must have said: 'Papa Stranger.' "

"If you want, we'll call them over."

"It's not worth the trouble. Tomorrow your mothers will realize they got the wrong name. Only strangers are to be welcomed in this way. Well they know that. Only strangers are brought meals. Even you know that."

"Yes, but they said: 'Papa. . . .' "

"Stranger."

"No, Papa Stay-Put."

Iguana-Son now ate before his friend. He licked his fingers, and he belched. Mouthfuls followed upon mouthfuls. And what beautiful aromas those dishes had! The hut was filled with their sweet smells. Kacou Ananzè told Iguana stories of times past. But Iguana did not listen to them; he was too busy eating, his eyes at half-mast, his nostrils quivering.

On the third day, Kacou Ananzè said to his friend: "Well! you realize, don't you, that your mother's funeral celebration is lasting a bit long. It's time for us to go back. Work awaits us; there's the harvest to gather."

"We did it before we came."

"I mean, we have those new fields to clear."

"It's not time for that yet."

"Soon, though."

Iguana gave a deaf ear. And the funeral celebration throbbed its hardest.

Again that evening, the young girls arrived with the dishes, and, as they set down what they carried, each one shouted out: "Here's the meal for Papa Stay-Put."

"Ah! Papa Stay-Put, Papa Stranger's friend?"

"No, our mothers told us: 'Papa Stay-Put.' "

"Come now, my children, you always have the habit of distorting. . . ."

"No, our mothers told us: 'Papa Stay-Put.' "

"Enough then! He's my friend. I tell you, our friendship is well known; we are cited as an example everywhere. Have you never heard of us? Why there's not another friendship like ours under heaven. Papa Stranger and Papa Stay-Put—they're like the fingers on a hand, always together. Isn't that so, Iguana?"

Iguana did not answer. He uncovered the plates, one after the other. Chicken, mutton, veal, pork, guinea-fowl. . . . And all of it smelled so good! So very good! And the aroma of all those dishes filled the hut.

Iguana ate. He was still eating when the drums sounded. Before going off to dance, Iguana placed one of his skins near the dishes. Kacou Ananzè also went off to dance.

Thinking to profit from the crowd's distraction, Spider ran into the hut. Those dishes were now his. But Iguana was over there, near them.

"What? You here? What are you doing over there? The food's going to get cold. You should eat it now. I just came in to find something to drink. . . ."

Iguana did not answer. And Spider left.

Iguana was dancing like crazy. Spider went back into the hut. But again, Iguana was next to the dishes. He went out once more. Iguana was still dancing; the women were waving to him, everyone was cheering him on. Truly, he danced well. And that is how he got the better of Spider. His friend tried to beat him again, but given the hunger in his stomach, he was defeated by Iguana-Son, who was carried around in triumph by the entire village. That very night the two friends left Mother Iguana's village. And that very same night, their friendship was broken.

THE PIG'S SNOUT

In the olden days the pig had a trunk, a fine trunk. But that was long ago, so long ago that the pig himself could no longer remember it. A longer and much more beautiful trunk than that of the elephant. Everyone admired this trunk, and everywhere they spoke only of this trunk, the pig's beautiful trunk. They spoke so kindly of it, in fact, that the elephant became jealous. And Kacou Ananzè also, because people even dared to speak of the beautiful trunk before the master of evil deeds, as if to say to him: "You've nothing that gives you any worth at all!" And what about his feats then? And his fabulous tricks? No, the people pretended to ignore them.

Kacou Ananzè was not the least bit resentful of the pig. And if he was finally forced to cut off that beautiful trunk, it was due to the following circumstances.

Kacou Ananzè's village was a large village, the seventh largest after those of the elephant, the rhinoceros, the buffalo, the lion, the panther, and the tiger. They were the seven nobles of the animal world. A pack bound together these seven souls who were forever obliged to help each other, day or night. Not a single one of them could undertake anything without first conferring with the other.

Ananzè could, at his leisure, dine at the lion's house, or at the panther's; he could sleep at the elephant's house and not be disturbed. The elephant could wallow in the buffalo's world and know that the ant would not dare to try and tickle the end of his trunk. The ant knew that such impudence would bring about the extermination of her people. And so, the prudent ant, aware of her weakness and careful not to rub shoulders with the nobles of the bush in any way whatsoever, remained at peace. Even when she happened to see the elephant wallowing some place other than on the buffalo's land, she quickly changed direction. "With the noble ones," she would say to herself, "you must always be on guard. After all, the scores of creatures hanging onto their tails and sponging off them—weren't they eager to testify to the worst of motives?"

And so the ant, who knew that she was hated by everyone, remained calm. And she had good reason to remain that way, for all those tiny animals were forever trembling. They lived in constant fear, which only aggravated their bickering even more. They trembled whenever the lion yawned. They trembled whenever the panther showed his claws. And they trembled whenever the tiger swallowed his saliva. Yes, those tiny animals were trembling all the time, some to guard their beautiful trunks, their crests, or their ears; others, to hold onto their finery, their coats and their beautiful tails. Every one of those tiny animals found a reason to explain away his shivering, to justify his attitude. And all of them, in silence, submitted to the right of the strongest, that is to say, to the right of the seven nobles of the animal kingdom. The favorite game for those seven powers was the hunt. They beat the bush in turns. Each day, therefore, the tiny animals in the villages trembled as much as those in the forest. For when the hunt proved meager, those powerful beasts did not hesitate in the least to slay the tiny animals in the village in order to keep up their reputation. And each one of them was determined to outdo the other when it came to the number of spoils. And thus went matters for years and years, until one day, when the buffalo and his family left for the bush and did not return. The others waited for them a long time, for two days, a moon, even five moons. They still did not return. Search parties were organized but yielded nothing. The bush finally had its revenge on their daily plundering. The buffalo and his family disappeared, and there was no trace of their hides. After having scoured the forest in all directions, the tiny animals, one by one, had returned to take their places beside their powerful masters. They had all acquired the habit, the habit men force circus animals to learn when they train, and tame, those wild beasts.

After the disappearance of the buffalo, the lion thrashed them for no reason at all; the rhinoceros disemboweled them if they were late; the tiger skinned them, as if to teach them to rejoice in the buffalo's death. And the tiny animals trembled more than ever. We will not even talk about the hare. He shook more than a leaf. The ant no longer left her house. Her delicate scent could have easily indicated the spot where the buffalo's corpse was. But . . . but . . . the noble ones would accuse her of having killed the buffalo and his entire family. She had become extremely prudent because stories about such happenings had given her mighty worries. Therefore, she remained ensconced in her hole, scarcely poking her nose outside.

A few days later, the lion and his family did not return. Even the lion himself, the king of the bush, had been vanquished by the bush.

The panther's turn came next, then the tiger's, the elephant's, and the rhinoceros's. A catastrophe seemed to have struck the realm of the noble ones, those seven powers of the bush. And it would never be possible to recover the remains of any of them, never.

Only Kacou Ananzè remained. But Kacou Ananzè was determined not to let himself be taken like that. The bush might well be the bush that takes the buffalo, the lion, the panther, the tiger, the elephant, and the rhinoceros, but that bush would never get him. What is more, the bush knew that. So Kacou Ananzè was left alone to indulge in his favorite sport.

One day, as the sun stood directly overhead, casting shadows at the feet of the trees and animals, Kacou Ananzè, tired from hunting, sat down at the base of a high mountain. He drifted off to sleep. While dozing, he seemed to sense something approaching. . . . He opened his eyes, and what do you think he saw? A genie with a nose as big as that, yes, as big as that, as big as a hundred silk-cotton trees all tied together, and as long, even longer, than ten mahogany trees placed end to end. And the monster breathed! It seemed that all the world's air rushed in and out of that unbelievable nose, for it made such a frightful noise! It was terrifying! It sounded like a crash, like thunder. Mountains were lifted off the ground, hills were thrown afar. Trees flew off, after being torn from their roots, and animals fell dead when the genie's breath would merely graze them.

"Hum! What a nose!" said Kacou Ananzè, laughing.

"I use it to hunt with," replied the genie.

"A nose to hunt with? My God, the world's certainly filled with strange things! And I thought I'd seen everything! What's that monstrous nose made of anyway? That strange and colossal nose that inhales all the air in the entire world?"

Kacou Ananzè climbed up onto it; he caressed it, stared at it, studied and examined it. And thousands of ideas passed through his head. The hurricane kept on blasting away around him. And he asked tons of questions of that other one, Kacou Ananzè did, because his mind was never at rest. The kind and obliging genie answered them all and laughed at his astonishment, laughing too at all of the epithets. And with every laugh, the mahogany trees with their upright trunks would take off in a direct line toward the sun; and so too those silk-cotton trees with their squatty trunks embellished over with enormous boillike thorns. All those gigantic hardwoods with their powerful roots were torn from the earth and flew off, pounded and pulverized. It was indeed an unbelievable nose, that monstrous nose belonging to the laughing genie.

He sent his children to tease all those animals who had escaped his fatal breath. Annoyed, the animals would say to them: "Ah! if only you weren't genie Papa Big-Nose's children!"

"Go teach them some manners," replied the genie. "When a child's rude, you need to correct him. Go on, correct them!"

And when the children rushed up to correct the animals, Papa Big-Nose went "*Han! houn!*" and all of the animals fell dead in the gust of air from the gigantic nose.

A fatal gust that raised mountains and changed the directions of rivers!

Kacou Ananzè fingered the nose; he thought, he calculated. Because Spider knew that he was hated so much, he kept his head working all the time, day and night, inventing new tricks to catch each and everyone in his net. His position as the king of evil deeds had made that necessary. When he slept, Kacou Ananzè Spider never closed both eyes at the same time. He always slept with one eye open.

Standing upright on the nose, he thought; he calculated.

Then one morning, after having reviewed all of his feats, he grabbed his head in both hands and said to himself: "Really now! how stupid it is anyway to chase after game all the time, especially since all you need is a nose and a '*han! houn!*' to get all the game you want. It's obvious that God didn't want me to have such a nose. But you can make a gigantic nose like that one, and a fatal breath too. . . . I'll make me one."

And gathering up all the animals that had been killed by the fatal breath, Kacou Ananzè returned home. He had scarcely arrived when he called together all the tiny creatures of the village. After lying down on his back, he said to them: "Go to the river and into the mountains, go anywhere you wish, but bring me some sand, and more sand, so that by tomorrow night I can have myself a nose as big, as enormous, as that mountain over there."

The tiny creatures bowed and then left. They returned from everywhere, from the mountains, the quarries, and springs, loaded down with sand. They mixed it with clay, erected scaffolding, and set about their task. They worked and worked some more, without a moment of rest, each one of them moving mechanically, like an automaton. They were dazed from work. And they had to finish that nose by tomorrow night, a nose as big as that mountain over there. Many of the tiny creatures fell from fatigue. But this nose must be finished. And they finished it. They finished that monumental, stonelike nose. All night long the fire was kept up to dry it. And the next morning, the nose was hoisted upon the shoulders of six hundred and seventy-five tiny creatures who set out for the hunt. Kacou Ananzè was proud to be the owner of such a nose. The whole bush looked at him: the birds, the insects, the trees. When the birds chirped and the insects whispered and the trees rustled their leaves, they seemed to be asking one another: "How long has Kacou Ananzè sported a nose like that one?" Ananzè appeared small, so very small, underneath that monumental nose. The monkey, rather insolent by nature, burst out laughing and leaped from branch to branch, after having apparently danced a few jigs on Kacou Ananzè's nose. And when the dragonflies got tired of flying around, they alighted on it. Despite the many teams of work soldiers that made way for this nose, the wicked liana vines kept thwarting its passage.

Finally, at the end of a three-day march, a troop of antelope was seen gamboling about in a beautiful clearing. Kacou immediately sent his children to provoke them. The antelope got mad and said: "Ah! if only you weren't Papa Big-Nose's children. . . ."

"Teach them some manners," replied Ananzè. "Correct them! When children are rude, you need to correct them."

And the troop of antelope began to pursue the tiny spiders. Kacou breathed his hardest: "*Han! houn! han! houn!*" Nothing. The antelope kept coming. Even the leaves stopped rustling. This troop, joined now by others, was getting nearer. And Ananzè threw himself under his monstrous nose that was being carried about by six hundred and seventy-five strong but tiny creatures.

"*Han! houn! han! houn!*" What a joke! Not even the slightest speck of dust fell from the smallest leaf. It was even calm in front of the huge nostrils where gnats were flying about. The birds chirped quietly, the monkeys continued playing, the butterflies kept on chasing each other. Dragonflies remained poised on the edge of the nose. Peace still reigned in the forest, at the end of that phenomenal nose. But the troops of antelope, now joined by several dozen others, kept charging.

"*Han! houn!*" The flies walked along the nostrils with perfect ease. They walked in and out of them, buzzing away happily. And the minutest particles that danced in the light's rays kept on dancing and spinning. The tiny creatures trembled, the nose trembled, and Kacou Ananzè also trembled. It was difficult to tell just which one of the three trembled most. And Kacou Ananzè, still trembling, said to those tiny creatures: "Don't move! Let's let the antelope approach, and then we'll see."

"*Han! houn!* Come on now, don't shake my nose! Will you please stay calm?"

And the antelope kept coming; you could almost touch them! Then Kacou Ananzè ordered a fast getaway. Everyone had been waiting for just that order. A stampede followed.

"Dig in! Dig in!" Ananzè kept shouting.

And the nose? What! Do you still want to talk about that nose that had been in ruins for so long now? That nose that fell apart in slabs whenever it wiggled on the shoulders of the panicked animals?

Each one went into the first hole he encountered. Often five, six, ten, seven, twenty tiny creatures took a hole by storm, then would leave it, anxious to get away, far away from those antelope whose breath they felt at the back of their necks.

The little spiders kept tripping their father who, in turn, tripped them. They would all roll on the ground, only to get up again immediately and run even faster, for already the antelope, the antelope. . . . Ay . . . faster! My God! The antelope . . . the antelope. . . . *Plouf! Plouf! Plouf!*

They sank into a hole, grabbing each other by the hand, or by the foot.

Ah! and it was time too! If the flight had lasted a bit longer, it would have meant the end of Kacou Ananzè and the spider race. The antelope had only to lift a foot to crush them, to lower their horns just a bit more to send them off to die in the trees. They even snickered, certain of their victory, when, at the last minute, Spider and his children sank into the hole.

The troop of antelope stormed around the asylum for a long time. They wondered how to go about capturing the spider people. They were considering this when along came the pig with his beautiful trunk. He was on his way to the fields, with a basket on his head, a branding-iron in hand, a pipe in his mouth, and flyswatters under his right arm. He came, "*clouc . . . clak!*" His short feet wore sandals made from the wood of an umbrella tree, and his pipe went "*poum! poum!*" The smoke that encircled him broke apart in streaks, and was then absorbed by the wind. The antelope said to one another: "Wait, there comes Brother Pig, and he has such a long hand too. He'll do the job for us."

"What's up?"

"What's up? It just so happens that some rather impudent creatures came into our most secluded retreat and provoked us. We're determined to punish them in such a way that they'll never forget it."

"So that's it, no one gives us animals any respect nowadays. We've got to make an impression on them and prove to all those hunters and other people that we are, after all, kings of the forest. But back to your point, where are those insolent creatures?"

"Inside that hole."

"And who are they?"

"Kacou Ananzè and his sons."

"Kacou Ananzè? Did you just say Kacou Ananzè?"

"Yes. . . . Kacou Ananzè."

"I'll get him, I will," said the pig, setting down his basket and his fly-swatters, his pipe, and branding-iron. "Would you believe that one day he even dared . . . this is going to take a long time to tell. Anyhow, one day, the very same spider who trembles in that hole had the gaul to eat a tiny piglet of mine. He was the most beautiful child that my wife, the sow, had just brought into this world. A sweet little piglet, who was very pretty, all pink, with shiny bristles. A dear of a piglet. Well, Spider proceeded to eat this jewel, this masterpiece of a piglet. Afterward, my wife and I couldn't stop crying; and since then, we've looked for a way to take revenge. . . ."

"How can we repay you?"

"Repay me? You were only provoked, but he ate my little piglet. . . . I'm going to make them come out of there. You'll soon see them at the end of my hand. . . ."

The antelope danced for joy, anxious to flatten Spider and his children, to pulverize Kacou Ananzè and his little spiders.

"Here's the signal to tell you when I've got hold of that scoundrel," said the pig. "When you see my tail"—and this pig had a truly fine tail—"go round and round like that, it means that it's done, that I've got him. Throw some clay on me, then, on my back there, as a sign of victory."

The proud pig bravely inserted his beautiful trunk into the hole. Kacou Ananzè, who anticipated everything, was preparing red-hot machetes. The trunk came down. It turned to the right. It turned to the left, and kept coming. It stopped a moment, then moved forward again. The little spiders blew on the blazing fire, and it roared. And the machetes became white. Ananzè watched as the pig's beautiful trunk came on down. The machetes kept getting whiter. They were as white as the noonday sun. Outside, the antelope were dancing and singing. They were going to get Spider. . . . They were going to purge the world of that hateful breed! The trunk turned to the right and to the left; it drew back for a moment, and then descended even further; it brushed up against a wall over here, paused before a crack over there, stopped for a second, as if to catch a breath, or to gather up its strength to make a decision, and took off again, stretching forever downward. The machetes were now whiter than the noonday sun. The trunk kept coming. Spider watched it come. Outside, the antelope were bathed in sweat as they danced under a fiery sun. But they kept on dancing.

When the beautiful trunk came within close reach, Ananzè took up one of the machetes, and "*chui!*" He cut off the beautiful trunk. And feeling the pain, the pig's tail began to turn round and round, like that.

"He's got them! Ah! he's got them!" shouted the enormous herd of antelope.

Clay by the sackful fell onto the pig's back. The tail kept turning, and the pile of clay grew higher and higher on the spine of that unhappy pig who trembled with pain, and who was more than eager to be far away from this infernal hole.

Finally, he managed to disengage himself. And what do you think the antelope saw? A snout. "What's that? Where's the pig's beautiful trunk?" the frightened antelope wondered, as they all took flight, leaving the pig to his fate.

The pig also started to run, and he kept running, since he thought that he was being chased by Kacou Ananzè who, tucked away in his refuge, treated himself to that beautiful, fat trunk.

And from that day on, the pig has sported the snout we recognize him by.

THE HUNTER AND THE BOA

A very poor hunter had set his traps along the banks of a river.

None of the traps anywhere had caught even the tiniest animal. Not even a palm-rat, hurrying to scramble up a palm tree to get at the finely ripened fruit. And not even a single scatter-brained partridge who, always traveling with a group, frisked about in the clearings and undergrowth!

The hunter was, indeed, a very poor man. Therefore, he had gathered up all of his traps and had set them along the banks of the river; for even those that he had placed in trees had never caught a single bird. The birds would fly over in squadrons to the nearby trees, and perch on the bent wood of the traps to give their concert. And the traps would remain that way, as they listened to the music of the birds. The traps had, in fact, listened to the music for so long now that they lost all interest in catching anything anymore. And so, they always remained bent. Did they perhaps understand all that whispering, and wailing, and shrieking of the grief-stricken bush as it rebelled against the hunter? Against man?

The hunter then went to set his traps in the savanna. They caught nothing. He took them into the forest. The traps remained bent. He took them into the newly burned fields; but the traps persisted in catching nothing. That is why he took them to the banks of the river, for it was there that all the animals came to drink. But the traps still caught nothing. The man was wondering where next to go when, one morning, he discovered that he had snared a boa. With spear raised, he was just about ready to finish it off when the boa said to him: "Don't kill me, Hunter."

"Why shouldn't I kill you? Do you let us go free?"

"Hunter, have I ever done wrong to anyone in your family?"

"Well what about all those men the boas keep killing?"

"Release me, Hunter. I know that you're very, very poor. For months now your traps have caught nothing. If you want to be rich, the richest man in the whole world, then unhook me."

The hunter set down his spear. He hesitated a bit. A thousand ideas passed and repassed through his head, like whirlwinds in a hurricane. "If this boa were killed, skinned, cut up, and dried, why, it would mean a fortune! If I listen to his sugary proposals, unhook him, and let him escape, what part would he play in the bargain? And what if he turned on me after I let him go? A boa is a snake. And you must always watch out for snakes." He raised his spear once more and prepared to strike.

"No, don't kill me, Hunter. Release me, and you'll be the richest man in the world."

The waters flowed by. Along the banks and in among the mangrove trees, they told a thousand stories to the immovable land, a land that would never travel to another region, but one that would always be crouching there, over the water, admiring her mop of hair composed of trees and weeds that were crawling with all the lice in the world, swarming with every vermin in creation. Stirring loose thousands of twigs along the banks, the waters recounted their adventures to an attentive land, a land fascinated by the exciting news that the indiscreet and forever-gossiping waters had picked up while listening to the conversation between the hunter and the boa just so they could repeat it farther on, as they made their long journey. The small fry pretended to quarrel over a piece of fruit, or an insect, and gave each other quick flicks with their tails. And one by one, the little waves made their way to the banks to deposit their cargo of twigs and to push their earlier loads farther up onto the land.

"You have your destiny right in your own two hands, Hunter. Whether you'll be rich or poor, happy or miserable, depends on you. Go ahead and choose."

"If I release you, will you harm me?"

"Since when have the bush animals behaved like you?"

"It's just that. . . ."

"We animals attack straight out, face to face, and we're even more direct when it comes to rewarding our benefactors. We've never envied their good fortune. And we've never been jealous of the positions they may have won as a result. On the contrary, the happier they are, the prouder we are. We like to show our good-heartedness. . . ."

The rope was pulled so tightly around his throat that the boa's eyes grew red, and redder still, as the blood rushed into them; they were so red, in fact, that the hunter could no longer stare into them.

"Go ahead and choose, Hunter. Today your fate lies in your own two hands. You can be rich or poor, wretched or powerful."

The hunter set down his spear and released the boa, who said to him: "Follow me!"

And the man followed him into the forest. They traveled through the forest of boas, and through the forest of genies, for there are other forests besides man's; and in those forests there were mountains, and rivers, and species quite different from those found in man's forest. And an undisturbed peace reigned throughout these regions. The flies when they swarmed made such beautiful music! And the breeze sang such charming melodies as it brushed against the leaves. Even the air that one breathed was so invigorating there. And a moss that was softer than cotton was to be found everywhere. . . .

They finally reached the boa's village. How many days, or moons, or years did the hunter remain there? He never could say. For when you spend a thousand years in that country, you think that you have only spent one! The fact remains, however, that when he left, the boa handed him two little gourds and said: "Return home. As soon as you arrive, throw this gourd to the ground. Keep the other one, for thanks to it, you'll be able to understand the languages of all those who live on the earth."

The happy man took his leave, eager to have charge of his own fortune. He carefully pressed the two gourds to his breast, which was beating with joy. He was so afraid that the boa might change his mind and come back to get the gourds that he almost ran.

As soon as he arrived home, even before he put down his spear, he threw the first gourd to the ground. And what do you think he saw? You can imagine what. A castle just like those he had seen in the land of the genies. And all the wealth of the entire world was there inside.

Our hunter lived happily now. And sometimes he would whisper to himself: "Poverty can force you to make such big mistakes! If I had listened to my anxieties and hunger pains, and killed the boa, would I now have all these blessings?"

The hunter had a dog, and this dog was friends with another dog, one that was mangy and without a master.

One noonday, right at mealtime, the mangy dog was sitting up there on his bottom, a bone between his paws, when he said to his friend: "Two moons from now we'll have a famine. Whoever wants to get rich should listen to me."

"And who's going to listen to you, my friend? You know very well that no one can understand our language. Would you like me to go into business?"

"If your master by chance. . . ."

"No, he doesn't understand."

"Be this as it may, if I had a master, I'd tell him to profit from the famine so that he could get rich."

"Get rich on another's misery?"

"But men do that anyway. It's the only way they know."

"Come on now!"

"But yes, I tell you they do!"

"You only make such remarks because you don't have a master."

"Me, with a master? What for? I don't need a guardian: I have myself."

"I have a good master who's been very generous ever since he returned from the boa's village."

"Even a good master is a crotchety master. You know that. I prefer the bush and freedom. I even prefer my mange."

Profiting from the conversation that he had overheard, the hunter bought and stockpiled an entire year's harvest. The famine came. The hunter resold his provisions to everyone at a higher price and, in so doing, became even richer.

The mangy dog came back once more and said to his friend: "Did you see what your master did?"

"What did he do?"

"Didn't you see the prices he charged for his provisions? I keep telling you that in the world of men the misery of one makes the fortune of another. And one thing more. In a month's time, all the young girls of the village will die. The only ones who'll survive are those who move to the other side of the river."

"Survive what?"

"Hum!"

"You can tell me, my friend. We'll keep it to ourselves."

"The plague."

Once again the hunter overheard the conversation, and after he had arranged for a beautiful house to be built on the other side of the river, he moved his family there.

The plague set in with a vengeance and swept away all the young girls of the village.

After the devastation, the hunter moved his family back, and since he was the only one who had young girls, he became the father-in-law of all the young men of the village. And he became even more powerful.

The mangy dog went back to his friend and said: "A fire will destroy the village. Your master's entire fortune will be the victim of its flames."

A fire did break out; it was terrible and pitiless. Only the aging hunter was able to save his goods, for he had heard the mangy dog's words.

"Your master understands our language."

"Men don't understand animals."

"Then you must be the one who tells him what I say each time I come."

"Why do you think I'm the one who tells him what you say? I've got a fine master; he's far better than any other man."

"Your master has managed to escape every hardship. That's good. But in a week's time there'll be a flood, a flood without precedent in this country. It'll be impossible to calculate the damage."

The hunter once more took the necessary precautions and suffered nothing from the calamity.

Both dogs began to worry. That man could understand their language, for sure!

Ten years went by. The village filled with people once more, and
resumed its old ways. Memories of past hardships became dim and
distant. Whenever someone mentioned them, a few thought they were
talking about things that happened centuries ago. Death continued to
claim a man here, a woman there. Let's not even mention the children.
Death is a glutton, a permanent calamity. She lives in every hut, waits at
every turn in the road, at every intersection, and hounds all men. She
walks with the young girls who go to the springs for water; she follows
the women who go to the fields in search of food; she accompanies the
fisherman when he throws his nets, the hunter when he scours the bush,
the traveler. . . . She stays awake while the rest of the village sleeps. And
she is still awake the next day.

Twenty years had passed since the day the hunter had released the
boa.

One morning, the same mangy dog, now mangier than ever, went up
to his friend and said: "Your master's going to die."

"What's that you say?"

"I'm saying that on this very day, precisely when the trees gather
their shadows up under them, your master will die."

"And how can he be saved?"

"Only by returning the second gourd to the boa. But if he returns
that gourd, misery will stalk him once more; he'll have to take up his
spear and visit his traps again. He'll be even poorer than he was before.
But he'll live for a long time yet. He must choose what he wants to do."

The man overheard the conversation. He was going to die. He
watched the sun climb the sky and creep up to the tree tops; he watched
it dwarf the shadows and move them over; he watched it pile them up
little by little underneath the trees, and he wanted to imprison that sun.
He went from the gourd to his wealth: to his gold, his diamonds, his
rubies, all radiating dazzling streaks of light. In the rooms there, they

seemed like mounds of glowing embers fanned by the wind. And it was
then that he really became conscious of how well-off he was. And the
higher the sun climbed, the more his wealth dug deep into his heart,
clung there, and ingrained itself.

He ran to the gourd, grabbed it, but put it down again.

His cheerful wives were talking and laughing in the courtyard. The
children were playing. He listened to their gay voices and his heart was
moved.

The sun kept climbing. Glittering fluffs of kapock scattered their
seeds and their featherlike flakes in the wind and were carried off. The
flowers smelled sweet. Bees were humming in the blossoming trees; butterflies were darting about and birds were chirping. June bugs perched
there for a moment, then left.

As if to make fun of the hunter, the mangy dog kept saying over and
over: "What's wrong with your master? Does he know that he's going
to die?"

"..."

"He must know, for ever since I mentioned to you that he was going
to die, he's totally changed his ways. We'll see if he has the courage to
abandon his wealth and become poor again, if he chooses to scour the
bush once more, with the spear on his shoulder. Let's make a bet."

"Why?"

"I, for one, contend that he won't have the courage to abandon his
wealth. That he won't want to live without it. But life is so sweet. . . .
Just look at the flowers, listen to their music, smell them. Could you give
up life as easily as that? Misery lasts only a moment; we must remember
that happiness is what endures: it's people living together in harmony,
it's a sense of well-being that's felt everywhere. . . . Your master sees
only his own little happiness. He thinks that his fortune taught him how
to appreciate life. Look at him there, hovering over his wealth. The poor
man."

And they both laughed, as the mangy dog kept on teasing and goading.

The sun climbed higher; the shadows huddled beneath the trees; it was just about noontime, the fatal hour. The hunter kept hesitating; he paced back and forth, from the gourd to his wealth, from his wealth to the gourd. He still hesitated, and the sun kept climbing. It was almost noon.

If you were in his place, what would you do?

THE SACRED COW

"And above all, Hyena, don't touch the heart. Do you hear me?"

"What do you take me for? You've said the same thing to me for ten days now! The heart! The heart! What would I do with a cow's heart? Even though my gluttony's legendary, I still have something upstairs here, in my skull."

"I must keep telling you again and again. The heart! Be careful of the heart! A bite here, a bite there, and with that lusty appetite of yours, an organ like the heart is hit fast. So watch out for the heart, Hyena."

"Listen, Kacou Ananzè, if you still want to take me with you, then take me; if not, leave off with all that fuss about the sacred cow's heart. Take a good look at me. Do I look stupid? And even if I do, am I really that way? Huh? Well, say something; you've known me for years and years. You've had ample time to study me, I should hope. Even our grandparents' grandparents were friends. My mother would often talk to me about our families back then. Our friendship's an old one . . . tell me honestly, then, am I really stupid?"

"Well . . . just don't touch the heart! A bite here, a bite there . . . you never know. . . ."

"Do you mean to say then that I really am stupid? Since our grandparents' grandparents. . . ."

"It's a simple recommendation, Hyena, my friend."

"And you're going to take me with you tomorrow?"

"I promised I would. And Spider keeps his word. I can assure you that we're going to have quite a feast."

"I'll dig in only that far. . . ."

"Be careful of the heart. . . . There'll be plenty of meat, so much so in fact that you. . . ."

"I told you, I'll dig in only that far. . . ."

The hyena's eyes glowed. Just thinking about all that meat made her swallow her saliva greedily, and it went *Klouc! klouc!* in her throat. And she whispered to herself: "Don't touch the heart! Don't touch the heart! The sacred cow's meat is better game anyway. And how delicious that meat will taste!"

The saliva in her throat kept going *Klouc! klouc!* Her hair stood straight up, as huge chunks of meat marched in procession before her eyes. A beautiful, sweet smell of tasty meat rose up from the ground, and her mouth kept opening and closing.

"The heart must be the best part. And that sneaky Kacou Ananzè wants to keep it for himself. Oh, we'll see about that! I may look stupid. But we'll see if I'm really stupid! . . . I'll be the one to eat that heart, '*kpa.*' I'll cut it out in a single bite, and '*klouc!*' I'll swallow it."

Our hyena continued on with this sort of monologue, extremely pleased that, for the first time in her life, she was going to succeed in playing a trick on Spider, that terrible Kacou Ananzè.

"Tomorrow I'll be the one who walks away the winner; and after tomorrow, the entire world will know that I, Hyena, beat Kacou Ananzè at his own game. He must believe those stories about our grand-parents' grandparents! Since when has the Spider family had ties with the Hyena family? Don't touch the heart! Don't touch the heart! Well, I'll be the one to eat that heart!"

The day seemed long to her. She kept wondering what the sun must be dragging behind itself in the sky to dilly-dally in the clouds that way. Her impatience was feverish as she waited for night to come, but it would not come. The sun seemed to stand still. Ah! yes, because the sacred cow was about to be eaten, the sun did not want to go to bed. And our hyena gathered up enormous piles of branches and set fire to them. The smoke would hide the sun, and night would come. But the wind swept away the black smoke, and the sun showed itself again, happily dragging its load across the vast blue yonder.

And the hyena, drunk from the smell of all that tasty meat, "*klouc! klouc!*" kept swallowing her saliva. . . . Finally, night came. . . .

And so it was that God had a cow. A beautiful cow; the most beautiful cow in all creation, and also the fattest. You had but to see her to know that she could only be the cow of a god. Kacou Ananzè was God's friend, and because of this, he was a very powerful creature and highly thought of too. The gates to paradise were open to him at any time. The guards could recognize him from afar by his retinue and the sounds of his horn; and even the gate-keepers themselves knew when he approached by the way he knocked on the heavy double-doors that were usually hard of hearing: a drum-roll, then silence, two "*toc! toc's!*" and a second, longer drum-roll. He visited God's house more often than did Gnaminlin-hakatiba-Swallow, the court bird, more often too than did Eboroakole-le-Butterfly, the messenger. In short, God and Kacou Ananzè were best of friends. And they would always go off together to see the most beautiful cow in all creation, the fat and shiny cow with the smoking nostrils and the tail that constantly twirled above her hindquarters. A majestic cow whom the flies and other tiny animals respected.

God did nothing without consulting Kacou Ananzè, whose advice almost always outweighed that of the other courtiers. If, since time immemorial, men have harbored a sharp grudge against him and have attacked him in every possible way, it's because they remember the day when the dog came up and announced: "We men will consent to die only if we are resurrected on the third day"; and they remember that Kacou Ananzè was the first to reply: "Excuse me! I beg your pardon! but the guinea-hen who left here just a moment ago already brought us a totally different message. The dog is nothing more than an impostor!" God assented and dismissed the dog.

But if people were happy in God's house, on earth there was famine. There was nothing more to eat. Nothing in the air; nothing in the bush; nothing in the water. Nothing anywhere. Everyone grew thin, except Kacou Ananzè. Even God, who sometimes glanced at him out of the corner of his eye, must have wondered: "How come Kacou Ananzè is the only one who doesn't grow thin?"

Guessing at the meaning of all those unspoken questions, Kacou Ananzè merely shook his head and smiled.

The hyena had no more strength to hold herself up, not even enough to drag herself along the ground. Kacou Ananzè, on the other hand, had cheeks that big! And what biceps! What thighs! . . . Oh! but no, never look up when you should look down! This must not be the same spider, or rather, Kacou Ananzè must not be the spider that God had seen when he asked: "How can hunger make you grow fat?"

God was bothered by yet another thing: his cow was getting thin, and he had taken such good care of her. Her rations were doubled, tripled, even quadrupled. But she kept growing thinner.

God looked at his cow, then at his confidant Kacou Ananzè, and said: "How does Spider manage to bypass the current direction of things? Did I let slip some life-giving secret that he uses to keep from getting thin?"

Kacou Ananzè no longer parted company with the sacred cow. He shed tears as he watched her grow thinner and thinner. And such a beautiful cow she was too, with her smoking nostrils, her tail always twirling above her hindquarters, her quiet eyes—eyes that seemed to cry out to the entire world! He doubled his caresses and his flattery. He touched her tail and rubbed her hindquarters; he passed his hands along her back, patted her cheeks, and wiped her nose. And his attentiveness drew him closer to God more and more each day. But also more and more each day, the cow grew thinner, while Kacou Ananzè enjoyed a rosy complexion and a voice that was bell-like and deep. His voice could now overpower the lion's, for the starving lion could barely even roar.

His secret? Here it is. He shares it with you so that when you find yourself in similar circumstances, you will be able to use it to weather the hardship. For as it is recounted during the night-time gatherings where we live, the famine will continue each year to wreck havoc on earth.

Every night, Ananzè would slip into the park through a crack; using a thousand clever ruses, he would make his way into the sacred cow's stomach. There he would eat his fill; then, from the same opening—he only had to tickle it a little bit—he would emerge. And God was truly bamboozled.

The hyena was dying of hunger, so much so in fact that Kacou Ananzè took pity on her. One morning, she said to him: "My friend, save me, I can't hold out any longer. Bring me a few bones tonight."

"There are no bones in God's house."

"How about some leftovers?"

"No leftovers either."

"Some decayed meat then?"

"Not even that."

"I don't get it. Everyone grows thin but you; and you grow fat."

"That's my secret."

"Will you show me what it is?"

"Gladly. But you mustn't touch the heart."

"What heart?"

"The sacred cow's heart."

"What are you saying?"

"That's my secret right there."

"Will you take me to it?"

"Yes, but don't touch the heart."

Night had come, and they were off. The hyena had waited impatiently for this moment, and with but one thought in mind: to finally be able to have a good meal and regain her strength. For two cents she would have passed her friend up and left him on the road. But she restrained herself and simply kept saying: "Come on, let's go! Let's hurry!"

Slackening his pace, Kacou Ananzè replied: "We're going fast enough. You know you have no more strength; and besides, we've got a long way to go yet."

And the hyena's only response was to growl. Kacou Ananzè came to a halt and said to her again: "Make sure you don't touch the heart."

And the hyena snarled: "*Kpehin* . . . understood!"

There they were, inside the enclosure, right next to the cow whose tail was twirling round her bony hindquarters. Ananzè tickled her you know where. She opened wide, like that, and they entered the sacred cow's stomach through that passageway. The feast began.

The ravenous hyena gulped down everything. She drank the fat and the blood as she would drink gravy.

Ananzè kept saying to her: "Don't touch the heart!" But she had become deaf. She ate and belched and kept eating. She was stuffed full, but she continued to eat.

"What are you doing there, Hyena?"

"Me? I'm eating."

"You're touching the heart."

"No, I'm not!"

She had no sooner said that when, with a shout and a "*klac!*" and a "*hop!*" she cut out the heart and swallowed it.

And the sacred cow collapsed, fell down, and died.

The news spread quickly throughout the entire world. Everyone knew how much God valued his cow. The occasion was thus suitable for headline treatment. And everyone came to grieve. Those who had no more tears, having cried them all, dabbed saliva around their eyes.

Everybody came except Kacou Ananzè and Hyena. God kept watching and waiting for them. He was especially waiting for Kacou Ananzè, his friend and confidant. But the friend and confidant Kacou Ananzè did not come. It was time to give the order to cut up the cow. And this was quickly done. After the skin was removed and the abdomen opened, the belly and bowels were then placed in a large bowl and carried off to the dumping ground by a band of urchins who were to empty them of any excrement.

One of the children grabbed the belly. It was heavy. He called two other children over, but it took twenty of them to carry it and throw it down. The belly burst open, *plouf!* and Kacou Ananzè appeared, with anger on his lips: "What do you think you're doing? Can't you see? You rotten urchins, you! Can't you see? Didn't you see me there? Didn't you see me looking for special herbs to cure the sacred cow?"

"We're sorry, Papa Kacou. . . . We're sorry, Papa Ananzè! We didn't do it on purpose. . . . We just didn't see you!"

"Ah! so you didn't see me? I suppose I'm someone that people don't see then? Well, you'll find out."

And Kacou Ananzè ran up to God and complained.

But . . . yes, still left there was the hyena who, with a *"klac!"* and a *"hop!"* and a shout, had cut out and swallowed the sacred cow's heart.

She tried to save herself. Some children fell upon her, yelling: "Here's the murderer! Here's the murderer!" Each one grabbed what he could find to bludgeon her with. They beat her on the head and on the kidneys, especially on the kidneys, for in the chase that followed, their clubs kept hitting her kidneys.

They fell on her kidneys so thick and so hard that they smashed them.

And ever since then, the hyena has looked the way she looks today.

THE BAT'S RELATIONS

The bat was alone all day and all night—so alone, in fact, that the solitude weighed heavily on her.

On some evenings she seemed to feel a heavy weight on her shoulders, in her heart, a very heavy weight. At such times, strange and silly ideas would pass through her mind, a thousand ideas all without shape or form, furtive and transient ideas that came and went; and in their coming and going they had hollowed out a groove in her little head.

The bat was alone and led a quiet life. She never picked a quarrel with anyone; she endured everything with patience. And many were the animals who esteemed her, for she would put up with their insults.

One time the starving lion, having just returned from an abortive hunt, ate up all her provisions. She could say nothing, for the poor little bat was so very much alone. Another time the panther played the same trick on her. And it is even said that one day, after she had snared a carp, the crocodile snatched it out of her hands, because, as he put it, the carp was not a fish suitable enough to grace a bat's dish.

And thus went life for the unfortunate little bat who had no friend to amuse herself with, no friend to confide her dreams in or to share her joys. But she kept her sorrow to herself. She lived in total solitude, completely shut off from the rest of the world. And is there a more wretched misery than that of never being able to confide in someone, even if the secret leaks out and races through the village or the town?

Never being able to confide in someone is like suffocating, gentlemen! It's like dying, ladies! It's as though you do not exist. People are vessels that need to communicate; they always need to pour out the excess of their feelings and impressions on others. But the bat lived alone with her joys and her sorrows; and they weighed heavily on her all the time, for she lived them alone and bore them alone. Take my word for it! How very much, indeed, she would have liked to have a friend to quarrel with now and again. A little peck here, a beat of the wings there. . . . Then the pouting, and after that the making-up, which comes like a benevolent wave after a severe drought. But the little bat remained alone, without a single friend who could give her the chance to love life, to know the joy of living that comes when two people are in perfect harmony. A true friend! And that means a lot in life. It makes a person. . . .

And the little bat had been thinking of only that ever since the lion and the panther had eaten all the provisions that she had so laboriously saved up. Weary of being alone, she said to herself one day: "It's wrong to be alone all the time. I'm going to link up with someone who'll rescue me in times of misfortune."

She went off to find the hedgehog and told him about the marvelous decision that she had just made. The hedgehog was very happy and, as a sign of friendship, gave her some hair off his head. After that the bat knew the value of life. Just imagine! A comfortable friendship, a warm and attentive one too! They were always visiting each other, always ready to satisfy the other's needs, always questioning and giving advice to one another! And then one day she said to herself again: "The hedgehog is certainly a good friend, but won't I benefit even more if I associate with someone else too?"

And she set off to find the monkey.

"Papa Monkey, as you see, I'm alone. Will you accept me as your friend? If you do, my solitude will weigh on me so much less."

"I couldn't ask for anything better. But if you become my friend, I wouldn't want you to be Kacou Ananzè's friend too one day. War is always about to break out between him and me. Someday all the animals must get together and decide which of us is the smartest, him or me."

"Why do you think I'd go and see Kacou Ananzè when I've just come to you and you've agreed to be my friend?"

"Here's a bit of my skin as a sign of our friendship. This way it'll be easy for me to recognize you. The person who wears my skin is another me and will be able to benefit from all my connections. But I tell you again that I don't like Spider. He keeps saying that he's cleverer than I am. Ah! but he ignores the trick I'm getting ready to play on him. It won't be long now before he'll fall on his head one morning, and. . . ."

Although she was very pleased with these two friendships, shortly afterward the bat went off to make friends with other animals, who gave her some of their scales, a few of their claws, a bit of their white tails. The bat had become friends with everybody. You might say that she now had very long arms, for whoever touched her, touched in one fell swoop the gamut of her relations, entire families, in fact, for she had many friendships that branched out and criss-crossed each other, so tightly were they interwoven.

And from then on, whenever she went from one house to the other, her friends would look at her in a puzzled way and wonder: "Who is that strange creature who looks like the bat?"

Feeling strong and reassured now, given all of her friendships, the bat conducted herself admirably.

But nothing under heaven is made steadfast, certain, or immutable. And despite the bat's glowing health, she fell sick.

The illness worsened, and she died from it.

Yes, the bat died. The news spread quickly, as does all news in the bush. It tumbled from leaf to leaf, glided from one ravine to the other, climbed up mountain after mountain, and was transported by the wind, the water, and the breeze; it was carried about by everything that rustles and whispers. All of her friends were informed.

The hedgehog was the first to arrive. He looked at the deceased and said to himself: "That's not one of my relations. Her head certainly resembles mine, but that isn't sufficient proof. My friend the bat wasn't built like that either." And he returned home.

Then came Papa Monkey and all those who had given her some part of their bodies. They looked at her, shook their heads, and, as the hedgehog had done earlier, returned home. This was not their friend.

And thus ended the life of the little bat. She had sought out the friendship of many animals, but not one of them would bury her. . . .

Over there, the sun shined brightly through the topmost branches of the palm trees.

On the other side of the sleepy rivers, which the sunbeams fanned as if trying to fire them up, revive them, and give them energy, lay the bat's withering body.

Birds were preening themselves along the yet-deserted banks, as if preparing to take part in the burial procession that would lead the bat to her final resting place.

The bat's body grew stiff. But the women were laughing and singing as they traveled the pathway leading to the spring. And the clouds kept changing shape and size over and over again, a thousand times over.

The bat's body began to decompose.

The *roniers*[1] fanned themselves with their leaves as they watched the bat's friends coming and going.

---

1 A tree common to West Africa, whose wood is used to make furniture.

The ring-dove carried the news to the mangrove tree that dozed along the water's edge. The mangrove stirred, perked up an ear, then two ears, and finally all of its ears.

And, at the edge of the water it pricks with its tears, the mangrove still tells the famous story of the bat who, in her final hour, had no friends for she had wanted them too much while she was alive.

THE YAM FIELD

The field stretched as far as the eye could see. And it belonged to Kacou Ananzè. The yam shoots gracefully twined round their supporting stakes and sprawled lazily over the ground like fat women in a king's harem; they crept up the trunks and stalks of the trees and maize plants.

Growing hither and yon were taros, gumbos, pimentos, round white and purple eggplants, and beds of sweet potatoes with dark green leaves. Mingling with all these were yellow-leaved peanut plants. It was truly a beautiful field, especially at sunset!

And all these leaves and stalks, intoxicated with fragrant new life and drunk with invigorating air, rippled under the caressing breeze.

Yet what airs those yams put on! With their loincloths turned up like so, and their silk scarves playing happily in the soft breeze like battle flags, you might say they were gallant young men off to see their lovers.

The yams affected all sorts of airs. Every day they would burst forth and parade around in new shades of color that, with each passing hour, took on yet other hues, depending on whether the sun was rising or setting, depending too on whether the sky was overcast. And the string beans and taros had their own special colors that whetted the appetite.

Kacou Ananzè never tired of looking at the yams, the gumbos, the taros, the peony-red pimentos, the string beans whose tendrils clung here and there to the stalks, the twigs at the feet of the always-gossiping maize plants, and the banana trees that were growing rapidly, their large leaves serving as parasols for the other plants.

In the forest, persistent curtains of mist broke through the clouds. Elsewhere, the sun seared the skin like a whip, penetrated deep into the body, warmed the blood, and beat against the skull as if to open it and expose everyone's thoughts to broad daylight. But it did not succeed in doing this and, instead, contented itself by making everyone perspire. There, between two clouds, the sun shined for a long time in the small valleys, happy to stretch and spread itself out, to track down the shadows, nibble at them, consume and dissolve them. Under the fiery charge of this heavenly body, the shadows were forced to take refuge beneath the banana leaves and the thick foliage of larger trees. Undaunted, the sun kept hunting them out, pursuing them, riddling them with holes that beamed with light.

What a sight! Butterflies fluttered about; they would perch on one leaf, brush against another, fly up, then down, take a nose-dive, disappear, then reappear. Some were white, others yellow, and still others speckled. Two, four, several of them gadded about in this way. Like vagabonds, they sang the joys of indolence, of whimsy, fickleness, and sheer laziness. They flitted about while mocking the burning sun who, most certainly feeling ashamed, had just hidden behind a mountain of clouds to take time "for some serious thinking," as people might say, before coming back out to cast its rays even more forcefully. But the gallant sun was not ashamed; it was laughing! It ignored the butterflies' persistent mocking.

The birds came and went, singing. The husks of the maize plants let their beards be combed by the wind which then carried away the tufts. And the yams shook their leaves which, beginning to dry up, signaled the impending harvest. The birds flew from the field to the trees and back again. They perched on the stalks, on the branches, on the twigs, and on the trunks which had continued to waste away ever since the day the field was set on fire. The smoke rose calmly in the air, forming circles as it crawled and meandered about over the ground, only to straighten up, curl, then uncurl itself, and straighten up again. And the dragonflies! They refused to linger on any perch at all, for they were always in a hurry to go somewhere else. Having left their business dealings too soon, they came up to you absent-mindedly and caressed your ears and cheeks. They fluttered for a moment in front of you, whispered something in your ear, then, after discovering that you were deaf and realizing that they had been talking with a stranger, "*zinn! zinn!*" in two strokes of their wings they were gone.

All the while the sun kept dispersing its light over the yam field that stretched as far as the eye could see, brightening up all the colors.

Yes, the yams were certainly spectacular! No finer yams had ever been grown! And all those who passed by the field could not hold back their jealous whisperings. It had cost Kacou Ananzè many months of steady, difficult labor to have such a beautiful field, and this the jealous passersby ignored. They saw the field but not the labor and the deprivations that you take on and submit to when you pursue an aim all by yourself.

But something prowled around in his head like some beast. It was pacing there under his skull. . . .

"Go ahead then! Follow the path with your finger. It's over here . . . no, over there. . . . What? Can't you see it? Can't you feel it? It's running about under my skin, under my skull! Ah, poor me! Poor Kacou Ananzè! Always somebody's victim."

He chased it away, but it found refuge in the back of his neck, then returned and settled under his forehead.

"But is what's always hounding me really there under my forehead? Go away! Go away! I don't want anything to do with you!"

"But yes, Kacou Ananzè. . . . It's possible. . . ."

"Come now! What do you take me for?"

"Yes . . . go ahead and do it, Kacou Ananzè! It'll be a new and glorious chapter in your life . . . a new twist to your character that'll make you a legend."

"Get away from me. . . . And what about my wife and children?"

"Come on now, Kacou Ananzè! You know very well that your wife and children. . . ."

"And then you'll say to me: 'And what if you eat all those yams by yourself?' "

"Yes, that's it! And such lovely yams they are, too! Just look at them. Look at this field, your very own field! Do you think it's really necessary to share all this with others? What have they done to deserve it? They merely helped you. And who did the tough work? You did, and no one else."

"You're right. . . . I was the one who cut down all those trees. . . . Why that's a good idea after all. . . ."

"What is? To eat all those yams by yourself, "*toh!*' just like that, without giving a single one to anybody else?"

"Nothing's more mouth-watering than a good dish of yams and mashed sweet potato leaves seasoned with some coarse salt that crackles between your teeth and, for that extra touch, a little bit of honey."

"You realize, Kacou Ananzè, that you're a gourmet!"

"And some good, bitter palm-wine that really grates the throat after you've eaten a good yam cooked in ashes—there's nothing like it!"

"About those yams, Kacou Ananzè! What if you were to eat them all by yourself, '*pihan!*' Just like that, without giving a single one to anybody else?"

Those had been Kacou Ananzè's constant thoughts ever since the yam leaves had begun to turn yellow.

"Yes, I must eat all of them by myself!"

Evening came, and a sad Ananzè went back to the house; he was sad because he had not yet found a way to eat all those good things by himself. He kept rummaging around in his bag of tricks. And once again, he found in that bag what he had been looking for ever since that morning when something began whispering in his ear: "And what if you were to eat all those yams by yourself?"

He was going to have to die. That was all there was to it. Yes, he was going to have to die in order to be able to eat by himself all those yams that were already being harvested, whose tubers were fatter than the thighs of overweight women. He had to die; there was no other way.

Kacou Ananzè and his family were out in the field one day. They had been working since morning. The sun had slowly climbed up to the treetops, reflecting like metal on the leaves of the banana trees. They continued to work despite the oppressive heat. Everywhere you could see skeletons of insects, ringlike fragments of centipedes, and the shells of snails and other mollusks that the flames had caught unawares when the field was burned. Here and there, the rain had hollowed out little trenches.

They were busy working when, all of a sudden, Kacou Ananzè fainted. His wife and children carried him to the village where he returned to his senses and heard his wife Colou say to Eban, his oldest son: "Your father is about to. . . . Do you understand?"

"Do you really think so, Mother?"

"Nothing good will come of this fainting right at the moment of harvest. I've never seen your father faint before. It's not even one of our family's diseases. Scabies, ringworm, a swollen stomach, perhaps, but fainting. . . . Hum! Let's keep our eyes open, my son."

"I'll do that, Mother."

The harvest was over. They had put the pimentos, the taros, and the gumbos on one side of the field; the yams, the string beans, the bananas, and the sweet potatoes on the other.

And there was Kacou Ananzè, falling sick!

"Eban," said Colou once again.

"I'm keeping my eye on him, Mother."

"Your father's full of tricks—he's the sneakiest creature in the whole world!"

"Don't worry, I'm of the same breed . . . and have always been able to read his game."

One morning, Kacou Ananzè said to his family: "I had an unbelievable dream last night. I'm going to die."

"What did you say? You're going to die? What will become of your children? and me, your wife?"

"Alas! my poor wife, I'm going to die. Somebody came up to me and said as plainly as I'm speaking to you now: 'Kacou Ananzè, you're going to die. And when you die. . . .' "

"Oh! Papa's going to die!" cried the children.

"Let me finish telling you about the dream. The voice went on: 'And when you die, nobody must wash or dress you; you must be buried in your field, near the yams you worked so hard to grow.' "

"What? I can't be washed or dressed? I can only be buried in my field? Never! And what about the cemetery where all my kin are buried? But the voice kept on saying: 'It's for your own family's happiness, for your wife's, and especially for your children's.' "

"And so I tell you that I'm going to die, and you must do what my dream last night told you to do. But wait! I almost forgot. The voice recommended that a mortar and pestle, a cooking pot, some salt, and some oil be placed on top of my tomb. Let's see, what else was there? . . . Ah! my memory's growing old! I think that was all.

"I'll be happy to die, really I will. At last I'll be able to silence all those evil tongues."

Two days later, Kacou Ananzè died. He was buried in the field near the yams.

The funeral celebrations dragged on in the village. Every night there was drinking, dancing, endless palaver, and even some brawling, for everybody had drunk too much. All of the village tom-toms were stretched to the breaking point, since everyone was so happy to have buried Kacou Ananzè. Instead of throwing a pinch of sand over the poor corpse, some of them had angrily and repeatedly thrown handfuls of dirt. There was no trace of sadness on any face. On the contrary, eyes were laughing and seemed to be saying: "At last! And it's about time too!"

The funeral celebrations came to an end. All of the tom-toms had burst, and there was nothing more to use to call out the people to drink.

Every night, Kacou Ananzè would slip out of his tomb in the field and stuff himself with yams. As he listened to the roaring tom-toms, he would say to himself: "Those poor, deluded people! Since when do you learn of your own death through a dream? Since when have people been buried in yam fields? And how could I, Kacou Ananzè, die like this, without even having tried to cheat death?"

After the funeral celebrations, the people returned to their planting, hoes on their shoulders and machetes in hand; they would take large strides so as to avoid being soaked by the dew-drenched grass. Over here, heads were bending under a canopy of foliage; over there, people were practically crawling under a tree that several years before had been blown across the road by a storm.

Eban and Colou went to the field like the others. The mounds of yams had grown smaller.

"Eban, I told you to keep your eyes open."

"They are open, Mother."

"Then what about those yams? They seem to be shrinking."

"But Papa's dead!"

"Who else would do this?"

"We'll soon find out. I have an idea."

Night came. The whole bush was asleep. The sated animals made no sound whatsoever. Even those who hunted for their food at night were nodding off. You could scarcely even hear the occasional hiccup of a parrot, the hoot of an owl, or the rustling of a branch that disengaged itself from another after enjoying an amorous embrace. Even the insects, those indefatigable singers, had lowered the pitch of their chorus, for they too were overtaken by sleep. Tired of struggling, the fruit had fallen to the ground under the weight of the darkness; and the trees no longer had the strength to shake about in the wind, which, having awakened with a start, continued on its journey. But unable to rouse the swell of tangled, shadow-covered tree tops, it subsided, for it was also overtaken by sleep. Only the grasses stirred, but not for long. The stillness had become so profound that nobody wanted to disturb it. The fireflies tried to set fire to this immense green forest that they pricked with twinkling bits of fire light, fleeting glimmers, and shooting stars. Some dreaming chimpanzees screeched; some monkeys answered: "*kpa koun!*" The quiet then returned, only to be disturbed by some watchful serpent in the undergrowth, a blind centipede ever on the march, the falling of a branch or a liana vine, or by the innumerable sighs and whisperings of creatures in the night.

Leaving his tomb, Kacou Ananzè proceeded toward the mound of yams. But there was someone next to it.

Kacou Ananzè snapped off a piece of a branch, but this someone did not move.

He coughed slightly and dropped a dead root. There was still no movement.

"Eh! Eh! And where are you off to this fine night, my friend?"

". . ."

"Why, that's it! You've come to pay me a visit."

". . ."

"You must have been charged with guarding the harvest. That's what I'm doing too. The elephants, buffaloes, and monkeys just adore yams, bananas, sweet potatoes, and taros; I'm forced, therefore, to come out here and chase them away. Ever since my death, I haven't been able to sleep. I'm awake every night. How about you? Can you sleep?"

". . ."

"Why don't you answer? I'll get angry. I'll hit you. Yes I will, you thief, you! You must know who I am! I'm Spider."

". . ."

"Why aren't you running away? Ah! you want to be brave. You must not know me then. I'm Kacou Ananzè! . . . I've already told you that. I don't like this kind of joke. Beware if I get angry. You still won't answer? . . . How rude not to answer an old man like me! Well then, take that! That'll teach you to come and bully me in my field!"

And *pan!* another slap.

". . ."

"How dare you grab hold of my hand! What nerve! Let me go!"

". . ."

"And what about my other hand? It's still free. . . . Watch out! . . ."

Pan! another slap.

"Ah, but you're going too far now. There's no limit to your insolence. We can kid around, but not that much. Grab both of my hands, will you! And what will you do with my feet?"

And *toc! toc!* both of his feet were seized by that someone who never spoke a word.

"Ah! I get it. You've come to provoke me. . . . But no one ever provokes me. You've seized my hands and legs now, so what are you going to do with my stomach?"

And *paf!* his stomach became glued to this thing that Kacou Ananzè took for a human being, but which was really only a scarecrow made of birdlime.

Day drew nigh. One by one, the tree tops shed their shadowy cloaks. Holes appeared in the dissolving gloom. The pagoda-cocks and the thousands of bush inhabitants greeted each other in their different tongues. The sun was climbing higher. A fine powder of dew still clung to the leaves. The noisy toucans swooped down on the ripening palm trees and wrangled over their seeds.

Ananzè remained a prisoner. And after rummaging through his bag of tricks once more, he pretended to be dead as soon as he heard his children coming. They shouted:

"We've caught the thief!"

"He looks so much like Papa!"

"But our Papa is dead!"

"Our Papa's not a thief!"

Colou came next. She looked at him. Ananzè opened an eye. He even signaled his wife who, with her hands on her hips, said to her children: "This man isn't your father."

"Well, what shall we do with him?"

"We'll burn him," replied Colou.

And they set fire to the twigs and dead leaves that were piled up around Kacou Ananzè's feet.

The smoke rose up. It entered into Kacou Ananzè's nose and ears. Poor Kacou Ananzè was suffocating. Suddenly, the flames struck. At first they were pink, then red. They licked him, brushed against him, clawed at him, then bit him.

What? Would he let himself be burned up like a palm-rat caught in a hole? Either he's Kacou Ananzè or he isn't!

Colou fanned the flames with all her might, as if the wind was not blowing hard enough.

The birdlime melted. Kacou Ananzè moved. He moved a leg, then an arm.

Wrapped in flames, he pulled himself from the stake, threw himself upon his wife and children, and dragged them to the stream that was flowing nearby.

Some of them were swept away; others floated on the surface.

And ever since then, spiders have been seen floating on springs, streams, and rivers.

THE DOWRY

Truly now! God sure comes up with some funny ideas now and then! Just imagine wanting a sample of everything that's eaten on earth! Can anyone possibly count everything that's eaten on earth? When you want to give your daughter away in marriage, you just do it, without testing people. I had to buy my way to God's youngest daughter. And today he's seeking a husband for his oldest daughter. He doesn't demand any dowry whatsoever; but he will only bestow the hand of this young girl on whoever succeeds, in a maximum of thirty days, to bring him a sample of everything that's eaten on earth. In the beginning, we all thought that the heralds were playing some kind of a joke; but when those same heralds kept repeating the proposition for four days straight, we had to accept it as real. Yes, there was no doubt about it. The proposition called for: A SAMPLE OF EVERYTHING THAT'S EATEN ON EARTH. This was a difficult test, to be sure, but who wouldn't want to be God's son-in-law? And everybody set about the task. Some snarled and showed their teeth, others their claws; some begged for mercy, but most started buying what they had to.

Like a very rich but very thrifty man, I didn't want to throw myself into the competition just like that. I especially didn't want to lose my reputation as a wise and intelligent creature. I saw how the hare and the fox, and even the lion and the panther were carrying on, and I hesitated. But when the desire to be God's son-in-law finally got the best of me, I said to myself: "You've got to compete; you've got to compete."

On the morning of the fourth day, after I had decided to cheat God and win his oldest daughter by trickery, I proceeded to the ocean's edge so that I could weave my plan without anyone bothering me. Where should I begin? In water or on land? I was caught at an intersection, at the crossroads of the two elements: earth and water. I looked at the starfish, the crabs, and the sea urchins. I remained there, staring into the ocean, listening to it murmur, letting myself be swept away by its booming immensity. My head was working at a feverish pace. The proof? All of a sudden I seized hold of a crab and took off. After I had roasted my prized catch, I made my way to the house of an old woman I knew, and I said to her: "Look at the beautiful crab I just caught."

"It is beautiful! Truly beautiful!" she said as she swallowed her saliva, her eyes glaring at it enviously, greedily.

"And good eating too, I guarantee you."

"That's for sure. Just looking at it makes your mouth water."

"For two months straight all I've been eating are those rejuvenating crabs. Just look at me a moment: my cheeks are taking on color and my strength's improving. Thanks to those crabs, my exploits are without number. Really, they have a marvelous effect on you."

And the old woman's eyes, riveted as they were on the crab that was browned just right, had become literally red-hot coals.

"You can taste it, my friend. You know who I am. . . . There's no need to stand on ceremony with me; and that makes for a far more enjoyable relationship between us, a feeling of brotherhood. Do you want some?"

"Yes," replied the old woman.

She grabbed a claw and devoured it almost immediately, so anxious was she to get her hands on it. But no sooner had she eaten that claw than I flew into a rage. And the old woman began to shake; her teeth were chattering. I rolled my eyes and shouted: "You old glutton you! I said you could taste the crab, not eat the entire claw."

"What's all this nonsense about, Kacou Ananzè?"

"It's not nonsense. You must give me back my claw—immediately. If not, watch out."

"How can I give it back to you when I've just eaten it?"

"That's your problem. All I want is my claw back."

We argued back and forth for a long time, and when we were tired of arguing, I grabbed hold of a chicken and took off.

The old woman came after me, yelling: "Give me back my chicken! You're nothing but a thief!"

"Give me back my claw!"

"Come back, you thief! Come back!"

I calmly continued on, singing:

> "Thief! Thief! You know you ate my crab's claw.
> The crab comes from the ocean.
> The ocean belongs to God who wants a son-in-law.
> And God is the one who put me in this world.
> I'm leaving! I'm leaving!"

The old woman persisted and kept ranting. But I kept going.

A sample of everything that's eaten on earth! Now to find all that would not be an easy trick, and I had to succeed in this feat without spending anything. So I kept on going. On the outskirts of the old woman's village, I came across a young girl who was in the midst of drying peanuts.

"Good morning, my friend. I've just bought this chicken. Come! Prepare it for me. We can eat it together."

"My goodness, traveler, how much you look like Papa Kacou Ananzè! Are you his brother?"

"Me? His brother? Never. A man as rich and important as Kacou Ananzè doesn't travel without an escort; nor does he travel as I do, with a chicken in one hand and a crab in the other."

"But he's such a sneaky one, that Papa Kacou Ananzè! At home in the evening, my parents are forever talking about him, describing him. . . . And when I saw you, I immediately thought of him."

"No, my sweet, young girl, I'm not Papa Kacou Ananzè. Ah! but I'm starved! I haven't eaten for a week now! Cook it for me, and quickly now, okay?"

The young girl went off to get some wood; she made a fire, then killed the chicken, plucked it, cut it up, and threw the pieces into a cooking pot. The pot began to boil. The steam raised up the lid, and the smell of fresh pimentos, eggplant, and onion mixed with the smell of the meat made me swallow my saliva. I certainly would have eaten that chicken dinner and drunk that sauce that smelled so good and made the air around it so fragrant. But there was God's oldest daughter to think about; and there was also the fact that I wanted to become God's son-in-law. What an aroma! The young girl partially uncovered the pot to let the sauce simmer, and I saw a chicken wing rise to the surface, then descend again after another piece had pushed it over. Then our little chef took the meat out. I was waiting but for that. She had scarcely swallowed a bite when I reared up and said: "Why you little thief! Are you eating my chicken? Do you know how much it cost me? Now you'll have to get me another chicken."

"Traveler-who-looks-so-much-like-Papa Kacou Ananzè, what's all this nonsense? You even sound like Kacou Ananzè. I simply tasted it to see if the chicken was done just right, to see if the sauce had reached that peak of flavor it should have, given this fine bird. All the chefs and cooks in the world do this. And well you know that!"

"I know nothing of the sort. I want my chicken."

"Wait a moment then, while I go and speak with my parents."

"Do you think I've got time to spare to wait for your parents? Your parents owe me nothing. They neither took anything from me nor did they eat anything of mine. Give me back my chicken at once; if not . . . do you see these arms? these muscles? . . ."

The young girl began to cry. I took the chicken and some peanuts, then started on my way once more.

The girl ran after me, shouting: "Bring me back my peanuts, traveler, bring them back!"

But I just kept going, singing:

> "You ate a bite of my chicken.
> The chicken was given to me by an old woman.
> The old woman ate my crab's claw.
> The crab came from the ocean.
> The ocean belongs to God who wants a son-in-law.
> And God is the one who put me in this world.
> I'm leaving! I'm leaving!"

And I left. I had to move fast now; the thirty days were about up.

You realize that to become God's son-in-law is not within everyone's reach, especially if it means bringing him a sample of everything that's eaten on earth! What don't people on earth eat? I'm well aware of the fact that they eat sand, and snakes, and a thousand and one different fruits, and fish, and shellfish, and crickets, and frogs, and palm-rats, and rats in the bush, and rats in the house. . . . And God wanted a sample of everything people eat. I was thinking about that as I proceeded on my way, when I met up with some blacksmiths who happened to have just put some hunks of meat and some insects onto trays. I set down my baggage and joyfully called out to them: "Gentlemen, gentlemen, gentlemen, good day to you!"

"Welcome, Kacou Ananzè. Where are you off to in such a hurry?"

"What? Haven't you heard the news?"

"What news?"

"Where have you been? What rock have you been hiding under? Didn't you know that God was looking for a son-in-law?"

"Yes, we've already been informed of that. Don't you see those insects and those legs of lamb over there? We're competitors too."

"Good. But I'm not."

"You aren't?"

"Not me! I'm sick and tired of God's crazy schemes! I've had so much of them that I'd even prefer to go to my daughter-in-law's funeral."

"But when did you remarry?"

"Two years ago now. And obviously, without a lot of fanfare. I tell you, I've had my fill of noise. When you get old, you often change your ways."

"You remembered us in your wedding toasts, didn't you?"

"Yes! Yes, of course! One never forgets friends like you. . . . We've always hit it off."

"Ah! good old Kacou Ananzè! And to think that some people find you difficult!"

"Those poor devils; they're merely jealous and envious. . . ."

"And liars!"

"And slanderers too! . . . With people as nice as you are though. . . . Ah! hold on! I was about to forget. I have some peanuts in my baggage there, and I'd like to have them roasted. Could you see to it for me?"

"How many are there?"

"That doesn't matter. . . . You know I don't pay any attention to such things; counting is not one of my habits. What's important as far as I'm concerned is that the nuts get roasted."

"There are thirty of them," said the oldest blacksmith.

"Thirty or thirty-one, what's the difference I say."

Reassured, the blacksmiths set about roasting the peanuts over hot coals, while I dozed. When I was awakened, the youngest blacksmith was standing right in front of me, wrapping my peanuts in some paper.

With a straight face, I nevertheless counted them. I was furious and said: "I'm missing a nut!"

"One more, one less, what's the difference?" replied the blacksmiths. They burst out laughing, obviously amused at the way they had returned the ball to my court. But one doesn't return balls to me like that.

"Excuse me, but this is a very important matter. Between thirty and thirty-one, there's a 'one,' and that 'one' counts."

"But you were right there when we roasted the peanuts."

"I was asleep until you came and awakened me. I must have all of my peanuts."

The discussion continued; the pitch grew louder on both sides.

I then lowered my voice, grabbed a leg of mutton and a handful of insects, and took off. The blacksmiths came after me, yelling: "Spider, come back! Come back, Spider!"

But I continued on, singing:

> "You ate my peanut.
> The peanut belonged to the person who planted it.
> The person who planted it ate a bite of my chicken.
> The chicken belonged to the person who raised it.
> The person who raised it ate my crab's claw.
> The crab came from the ocean.
> The ocean belongs to God who wants a son-in-law.
> And God is the one who put me in this world.
> I'm leaving! I'm leaving!"

And I kept going, spurred on by the desire to become God's son-in-law. I then met up with a palm-tree climber, a fisherman, a farmer, a black monkey, a red monkey, a lion, a parrot, a hunter, some fruit trees, and several genies and phantoms. I said a friendly word to everyone, man, plant, and insect alike, and managed to extort from each of them what I wanted and needed. In this way, before the thirty days were up, I had appropriated a sample of everything that's eaten on earth. I was proud of my feat.

And with a train of porters behind me, I then found myself on the road to God's house. God watched me approach. He thought he was making me afraid by staring at me like that. I finally arrived, sat down, and told him the news. He offered me something to drink. Proud of my accomplishment, and looking at him out of the corner of my eye, I drank some. Hadn't I succeeded in gathering up a sample of everything that's eaten on earth? But that must not have pleased God very much, for he didn't want his oldest daughter to marry Kacou Ananzè. With my legs crossed, I leaned back in my armchair, calmly smoking my pipe and savoring my victory. And then, as if surfacing from a dream, I said: "I've brought everything you asked for."

His only response was to see to it that I was well housed and well fed. And so, for three days I was the happiest creature in the world. However, I was beginning to get impatient when, on the fourth day, very early in the morning, God called for me and said: "Kacou Ananzè, all you did was to go to the ocean's edge and get a crab to procure all these samples that you've brought me. You are a clever one—that's for sure. I congratulate you. As far as my daughter's concerned, however, I can't give you her hand in marriage."

"But why?" I exclaimed.

"You didn't come by these things honestly."

"Didn't I bring you a sample of everything that's eaten on earth? Didn't I?"

"You stole the chicken from an old woman, the peanuts from a young girl, the insects and mutton from three poor blacksmiths. . . . You caused tears everywhere you went."

My heart was heavy. It pained me to hear such remarks.

"Is there something missing that explains why you refuse me your daughter's hand?"

"Look for yourself and see if anything's missing."

I looked around and searched through the bags to see what was missing.

"We're not living in a time of famine. . . ."

"But do they eat them, yes or no?"

And that is why I wasn't able to marry God's oldest daughter. I had forgotten to bring some tasty roasted flies.

SPIDER AND HIS SON

Kacou Ananzè had a monster of a son. He went to bed late and he got up late. Moreover, he knew absolutely nothing about anything when it came to using his ten fingers. His sole preoccupation was playing around, after which he would slump to the ground and begin snoring. And then he would snore some more. Reprimands of any sort had no effect upon him. He would just laugh in your face, scoff at you, and then walk away, his feet twisted out sideways, his legs bowed, and his head hanging crookedly to one side. He walked as a drunk man would.

You should have seen him sitting beside the fire during the evening, his knees level with his neck. He would just sit there, embracing the flames with his spindly arms. And Kacou Ananzè would stare at him and wonder: "That's a son of mine? How could he, Kacou Ananzè, known throughout the world as the master of deception, as the most intelligent creature alive, have a son like that?"

One day when he returned from his habitual walk, he again dropped to the ground and began snoring. Kacou Ananzè looked at him and saw red. And grabbing him forcibly by the shoulders, he said to him: "Go home to your family. I'm no longer your father."

"To what family? And who then is my father?"

"Let's not discuss it. I simply want you to go home to your family."

"To what family, Papa?"

"Impertinent creature! Do you still dare to speak to me when I've just ordered you to leave?"

The brat wanted to lie down again, but Kacou Ananzè grabbed him with his two hands, like that, and after turning him round and round over his head a few times, threw him way, way over there, shouting: "Go home to your family; you're not my son. You . . . you'll never be a Kacou Ananzè!"

Yes, Kacou Ananzè threw him out. But why?

A famine existed at the time. There was nothing left to eat in the bush, nothing in town. The anguish was the same everywhere. There was not even a drop of water in the springs and rivers; and no matter where you went, the sky was swept bare of clouds and arched over the land like an incandescent dome. The blazing sun even made the oceans steam. The sand was scorching hot everywhere: in the bush, in the villages, and on the river banks. You could see flames rising up, wriggling and slithering about, then dropping away as if they too were overcome by the heat.

Survival had become the concern of everyone. And feeding a family was a tremendous problem at such times. Spider-Son had let his father assume the entire burden of feeding and maintaining the family. Every time Kacou Ananzè would say to him: "Come, let's go look for something to feed our family," he would reply in harsh, nasallike tones, "What family?" You should have heard him say that—such smugness! And whenever Kacou Ananzè managed, by a thousand clever ruses, to bring something home, this do-nothing child was the first to come up to him, extend his hand, and snort: "Where's my share?"

His share! Do you hear that? His share! Ah! but you must be patient. Ananzè gave him "his share," and he ate it greedily. Afterward, Spider-Son would drop to the ground and start snoring.

Kacou Ananzè looked at him and wondered: "Can this boy be my son? This boy who has no get-up-and-go whatsoever, who has no ability to deceive, who's not even the least bit bright?" And that is why an exasperated Kacou Ananzè had said to his son that day: "Go home to your family. I'm no longer your father."

And he grabbed him with his two hands, like that, and after turning him round and round over his head a few times, he then threw him over there, shouting: "Go home to your family; you're not my son!"

He threw him far, far over there, beyond the dumping grounds that no longer existed, beyond the sun-charred forests and the exhausted springs, even beyond the blazing hot oceans, a long way off, way, way over there. He never knew what special force carried his son that far away. He just watched him go, further and further. . . . And you would have thought that he would go on forever. . . .

Finally, on the evening of the third day, the boy found himself in a magnificent forest that neither human eye had seen nor foot had trampled—a wondrously enchanted forest, all fairy-tale-like with its grassy-green carpet and its thousands of different smells. Springs babbled softly as they rolled over little white pebbles; the reeds and grasses dotting their banks wrote who knows what messages in the clear flowing waters; multicolored fish in cheerful little groups came and went with nothing to fear. The ever-mercurial birds seemed to magically change their attire as they twittered among the various colors of the branches. When they flew up, some of them would unsettle a few leaves which would then come tumbling down like flakes of gold. Spider-Son looked about; he listened. There was a noise behind him. He turned round, and what do you think he saw? A boa. Yes, a boa that he had mistaken for a mountain lying there beside the trickling springs. He wanted to run away, but the boa was quietly asking him: "What are you doing in my kingdom?"

And without omitting a single detail, Spider-Son told him what had happened. He told him about the disappearance of the white clouds that during the evening hours were fringed with an entire spectrum of soft colors ranging from pink to mauve to violet; he told him about the death of all the flies, and about his father Kacou Ananzè's anger.

The boa then said to him: "Stay here with me."

And Spider-Son stayed with him. He was so nice that the boa developed a strong affection for him and said to him one day: "Would you do anything I asked you to do?"

"Anything."

"Then close your eyes. Now open them."

Spider-Son closed his eyes. When he opened them, he was astonished at what he saw. His eyes grew bigger and bigger. Villages and palaces stretched out before him as far as he could see; everywhere there were fields and more fields of diamonds and turquoise and rubies, fields of every precious stone in the world. And all of those stones just lay scattered there on the ground.

"Close your eyes again. Now open them."

Again Spider-Son closed his eyes, and when he opened them this time, he was stupefied, even dumbfounded. There he was, inside a castle made entirely of diamonds, with gold ceilings, and stairways carved out of turquoise. To tell the truth, it was the most magnificent castle the world had ever seen. Everywhere there were armies and armies of servants and vassals. Even the trees, the mountains, the rivers, and the earth were made of gold; they sparkled in the sunlight and twinkled under the bright moon at night. And Spider-Son himself had changed. He was no longer that strange little creature with the crooked feet but a fine and handsome young lad aglow with health. His wives? Could one even begin to count them? And were they beautiful? Words could not describe them.

Spider-Son wondered if he was dreaming, if reality was truly that which stood before him, or if he was not, in fact, under some sort of spell. Was this a mirage? a hallucination? He rubbed his eyes. No, he was not dreaming. The boa was there beside him, laughing at his bewilderment.

"This is not a dream. You really have become the richest and most powerful king on earth."

However, as is the case with any miracle performed by genies, there is always a "but," always a condition. Spider-Son must make sure that his benefactor is never seen by anyone. He therefore hid the boa in one of the most secluded rooms in the castle.

Spider-Son ruled the happy nation for years and years. There was always an air of festivity about. The reputation of this good and power-ful king had traveled throughout the world. The wind and the swallows sang his praises at every moment during their long excursions; the geese and herons that hopped about on the banks of the golden rivers sang only of his wisdom. The monkeys, as they leaped from tree top to tree top, were careful not to disturb the air that the king would soon be breathing. And night and day the flowers would change their dress, for they no longer knew precisely what they should wear in order to keep the attention of their powerful master. Even the heavens draped them-selves in their most pleasant and enchanting colors, in exquisitely dap-pled tones and captivating hues. And the twinkling stars were like magic in the sky.

Spider-Son's ships traveled the oceans. Wealth flowed in from all sides, in gratitude.

Elsewhere, however, the famine raged on without interruption. One no longer knew from where she drew her increasingly destructive powers. Unable finally to hold out any longer, Kacou Ananzè decided one day to leave. But where should he go? There were burning sands and flaming oceans as far as the eye could see. Then one morning, a swallow flew by in the blazing heavens and spoke of Spider-Son's kingdom.

"Spider-Son! Spider-Son! That must be one of my offspring," Kacou Ananzè said to himself. . . .

And anxious to see this kingdom, he took the path straight ahead of him, walking in the direction he had thrown his son whom he had watched disappear in the distance. He kept walking, grinding his heels forward all the time. He encountered no one, not a single living soul. There was desert in front of him and desert behind him; there was burning sand on his right, a flaming ocean on his left, and a blazing sun overhead. He felt the heat waves all around him; they would arrive in gusts, blown over by a white-hot wind. . . .

Look over there, along the horizon! Do you see? What is that? A mirage? A long wall of greenery came into view, a forest that had been miraculously spared from the sparks of lightning in the sky.

And gathering up his courage in both hands, Kacou Ananzè ran toward the haven that was silhouetted before him.

He had scarcely set foot in this paradise when he fell to the ground, unconscious. When he awakened, he found himself in the most magnificent castle he had ever seen. And whom do you think he saw bending over him. His son! that very same son he had thrown out one morning after saying to him: "Go home to your family; you're not my son." They embraced each other to the point of suffocating. Ananzè was carried away with joy and kept hugging this son who was now so worthy of him, this offspring who brought so much glory to his race. They lived together happily. But Kacou Ananzè would often wonder: "How did my son go about getting so much wealth?" The origin of this vast fortune haunted him night and day. In fact, the desire to learn the origin of this fortune had become an obsession the very first day he set foot in his son's kingdom. And this obsession kept hounding him. He would chase it away, but it kept coming back to pester him. It was at his heels when-ever he ate; it was there when he slept. Never had he encountered an obsession as stubborn as this one.

He questioned his son's servants, but, as if struck dumb, they said nothing. Their silence roused his curiosity.

One day, the king decided to tour his estates. After all, it is tradi-tional for great folk to roam their lands. His subjects wanted to see him, or so they said. The preparations were scrupulous, down to the last detail; and everyone awaiting his arrival on the road ahead cooperated in the effort to win over this king whose praises they all sang. The day of departure arrived. The procession left without Kacou Ananzè, who could not shake that obsession of his. It marched forth, to the sound of fifes, flutes, horns, and drums. The precious stones that were scattered about everywhere radiated dazzling flickers of light. The flowers gave off their most pungent fragrances; the air was sweet and brushed against the skin like amorous caresses that were short of breath; and the sky displayed a beauty and splendor unheard of before. And every-where there was music, the music of the stones, the music of the flowers, the music of the birds, the trees, the insects, the grasses, and the shrub-bery; you could hear the sweet singing of the forest creatures and the love songs of the waters. Dragonflies and butterflies were also singing, accompanying the barcarole of the breeze as it rustled among the foliage.

Kacou Ananzè was alone in the castle. And his obsession was prey-ing on him even more ferociously than before. Deciding to get rid of it once and for all, he proceeded to scour the castle. He went in one door and out the other. He found an entire little city between those castle walls. . . .

Kacou Ananzè soon found himself in front of a small door. He tried to push it open; it resisted. None of his many keys fit the lock. He forced it open, and what do you think he saw in that room which was piled high with wealth? A boa, whose mouth was chock full of stones in every conceivable color. He grabbed a piece of wood and *pan! pan! pan!* banged it over the boa's head. The boa slapped his tail against the wall to his right, and the kingdom disappeared; he slapped it against the wall to his left, and the castle vanished.

Kacou Ananzè found himself naked once more, so naked, in fact, that he clung like a burr to the leaves.

And ever since then, he has been waiting there for the return of his son who, one day long ago, left to visit his kingdom from that very spot.

THE MAN WHO WANTED TO BE KING

Once upon a time there was a man who wanted to become king. Morning and evening, day and night, he thought of nothing else.

Every morning this dream would assert itself a little bit more.

And every evening it would become a little more ingrained in him.

The dream was so firmly rooted in his being that one morning he left to find God. This ambition had given him so much courage that he simply went up and said: "Gnamian,[1] make me a king."

"Are you unhappy with your present state?"

"Make me a king."

"Why do you want to be a king?"

"Because I want to, that's all."

"Ah! And how long have you had this desire?"

"For moons and moons now, for years and years, for so many moons and years that I wouldn't know how to even begin to count them all."

"Being a king is a heavy burden."

"The others aren't dead yet. Quite the contrary, in fact."

1 God in the Agni dialect.—Dadié's note

"But why do you want to be a king?"

"So that I too can know freedom and be respected as a man."

"You must think that one can be a man only if he's sitting on a throne?"

"I just want to be a king."

"But all those nonentities who are carried around in hammocks with crowds of people in front of them and crowds behind them aren't necessarily kings. Being a king is a very heavy burden. Are you so sure you want this?"

"Yes, I want to be a king."

"You must render justice; you understand that, don't you?"

"I'd know how to do that."

"True justice? The kind of justice that seeks out the truth and therefore acquits or condemns without any other consideration?"

"I'd know how to render true justice."

God looked at the man who wanted to be a king, smiled, and said to him: "Go back home now. Think it over again carefully, and come see me in three days."

"But I've already thought about it for a long time. I want to be a king."

"Go on home anyway."

The man left. But the more he walked, the more he longed to be a king. It seemed that everything around him—the wind, the trees, the birds, the grasses, the springs, even the insects—were saying to him: "Be a king! Be a king!" And he saw himself being carried around in a hammock with crowds of people in front of him and behind him, with crowds even to the side of him.

The three days he spent thinking about it seemed like moons and moons, years and years.

On the fourth day, before the roosters had even greeted the morning, before the moon had even been eclipsed, the man was already at God's door: *toc! toc! toc!*

"Who's there?"

"It's me."

"Who?"

"The man who wants to be a king."

"You're determined then?"

"Yes, I'm sure."

"And you'll be just?"

"Yes."

"Are you ready then to do what I shall ask of you?"

"Ready."

"Go and take a good look at this world; then come back and tell me what you saw."

The man left. He visited cities and hamlets; he roamed the bush. Everywhere he went, he witnessed angry discussions and trials of one sort or another. He saw men rendering justice; he saw the animals and plants rendering justice. He even saw the waters and the insects and the rocks rendering justice. He went from one marvel to the next. All creation lay revealed before him. His faculties were free to wander; he dug deep into the heart of nature and discovered the unseen bonds that exist between all creatures. He felt at peace with himself. He thrived. He had never suspected that the plants and animals, the insects, waters, and rocks were just like men; they too had a voice and were capable of rendering justice. Every day he felt closer to all those special kingdoms he loved and respected. And the more he traveled, the more he lost his desire to be a king. But he continued on anyway. It was as if he were being drawn forward by some special power. If, in the city, he felt oppressed, out in nature, he blossomed. . . .

An argument had broken out between the monkey and the lion. The lion was wrong. He knew that he was wrong, but he kept waiting there, sharpening his claws, for someone to be bold enough to tell him so. The elephant presided over the dispute; beside him were the buffalo, the wart hog, the panther, and the tiger. The panther was busy arranging his whiskers, while the lion, who pretended to mimic him, braided his mane. He kept yawning and wanted to shout: "I'm hungry!"

Everyone awaited the verdict in agonizing silence. The elephant scratched his head with his trunk, searching for the proper form in which to pronounce the sentence. His tiny eyes glowed in their sockets; they were glowing so brightly that the discerning monkey understood what was coming and slipped away.

They decided against him, since he had defaulted by leaving the proceedings.

Another time it was the elephant who complained. He had been stung by the ant, a very small ant who was trembling all over as she stood before the assembled masters of the bush with their claws and long sharp teeth in clear view. The entire insect world was petrified and remained quite still as it faced the huge mustaches and manes belonging to those all-powerful masters of the bush.

The elephant lifted up his foot so that all could see the large, suppurating wound. He alleged—and he had witnesses to back him up— that it was the little ant who had stung him. The ant, because she was little, was convicted of the charge. No one wanted to even listen to her. She was a habitual offender anyway. She always stung you, no matter if you were lying in wait for her or if you were sleeping! Everyone bore a grudge against her. If not her, it was the horsefly who played those games. But then again, the horsefly was considered one of the nobility.

One day the river filed a complaint against the stream because the stream kept singing a song that was similar to his, a song that he had inherited from his ancestors. Does the soft murmuring of a stream over pebbles and stones as it wanders among the trees resemble the monotonous voice of the river rushing to pay court to the ocean? A stream merely plays with the grasses and branches; the river, however, uproots them and drags them away with him. Could these two songs really be the same?

The stream just glides along like a vagabond; she turns round on herself, snuggles up against a tree lying across her bed, enters a small cave to learn a new song, and plays quietly in among all the shadows and light spots with the shellfish, the butterflies, the dragonflies, and the insects. She serves as a mirror for all the trees, liana vines, and birds, for the sun and the moon too, and also the stars, and the bright blue sky. She deposits a water lily over here; over there she takes away some duckweed. . . . She carries with her the laughter of young girls, the songs of washerwomen, and the whisperings of bamboo trees and reeds. And she never brings tears to the eyes of any society or family. She knows men too well to create new worries for them. After all, doesn't everyone come by each day to share a few thoughts with her, to reveal a little of what they are suffering? And murmuring quietly, she offers fresh, cool water. Despite the fact that this song in no way resembled the song of the greedy and pitiless river whose victims were always trailing behind him, the stream was found guilty. And ever since then, she has taken her waters and her song to the river.

The man continued his journey. He had seen some chimpanzees hide earthenware pots full of gold in the hollow of a large, flat root; he had seen a woman come and take a few of the pots and then leave; he had also seen a man come and take some. And he had seen the chimpanzees return and complain of the robbery. They saw a man standing near the hiding place, but they did no harm to him at all.

Another time, a man who looked almost exactly like the one who had taken the chimpanzees' gold cut down a palm tree to extract the sap. Some chimpanzees came up to drink of the wine. When the man came back and saw a chimpanzee nearby, he accused him of stealing and shot him. The other chimpanzees said nothing.

The man who wanted to be a king walked on.

It was so hot that day that the leaves did not even stir. The insects had stopped humming. The birds were still. Everything was quiet, deadly quiet. From time to time, a leaf, overcome by the heat, broke away and fell onto a carpet of moss. And the wind kept fanning the flames that burned the skin. . . .

The man was tired. He had walked to the edge of a river whose water was white-hot as it flowed by like glass under the ferocious sun. A kingfisher hovered overhead; and even higher than the kingfisher, very high in the sky, an eagle was screaming: "*San-Ehoué! San-Ehoué! San-Ehoué!*"[2]

The man climbed a tree to get some rest. He had scarcely begun his climb when along came another man who looked exactly like the one with the palm-wine, the one who had shot the chimpanzee. He fastened his shoulder-pouch to a branch and went for a swim. He swam for a long time, and then left, forgetting to take his bag.

A chimpanzee came along soon afterward, beating his chest as if to say: "I am the man of the forest." He too swam and played for a while; and then he saw the bag. He took it down, opened it, and began scattering the nuggets of gold he had found.

The man came back to get his treasure; he saw another chimpanzee and accused him of stealing. They began arguing.

From that day on, the chimpanzees of the city, the men, and the men of the bush, the chimpanzees, had, indeed, a conflict to resolve. The animals were uneasy, for the matter was brought before them.

---

2   "Only death!" Implication: only death can vanquish me.—Dadié's note

The man who wanted to be a king ran immediately to God.

"What did you find?"

And without omitting a single detail, the man told him everything he had seen.

"And what was the animals' verdict?"

"I left before they had given it."

"Go back then and bring me the verdict. And afterward I'll make you a king."

The man who had wanted to be a king, who had felt that he could render true justice, left and never came back. And the animals have not yet given the verdict in the case between the men of the city and the men of the bush.

They continue to investigate the matter and have now come to ask you what verdict you would give.

Meanwhile, God is still waiting for the man who wanted to be king. And he will be king, whoever brings the animals' verdict to God. Would you like to be this happy man?

Abidjan, July 3, 1953

OTHER WORKS BY
BERNARD BINLIN DADIÉ

Novels

    Climbié (Paris: Seghers, 1956)
    Un Nègre à Paris (Paris: Seghers, 1959)

Travel

    Patron de New York (Paris: Présence Africaine, 1964)
    La Ville où nul ne meurt (Paris: Présence Africaine, 1968)

Poetry

    Afrique debout (Paris: Seghers, 1950)
    La Ronde des jours (Paris: Deghers, 1956)

Tales and Poems

    Hommes de tous les continents (Paris: Présence Africaine, 1967)

Tales

   Légendes africaines (Paris: Seghers, 1954)
   Contes de Koutou-as-Samala (Paris: Présence Africaine, 1982)

Plays

   Monsieur Thôgô-gnini (Paris: Présence Africaine, 1970)
   Béatrice au Congo (Paris: Présence Africaine, 1971)
   Sidi Maître Escroc; Situation difficile; Serment d'amour (Paris: Présence
   Africaine, 1971)
   Iles de tempête (Paris: Présence Africaine, 1973)
   Mhoi-Ceul (Paris: Présence Africaine, 1979)